Moody Nolan
DESIGN

VOLUME 2

ORO
EDITIONS

ORO Editions

Publishers of Architecture, Art, and Design
Publisher: Gordon Goff

www.oroeditions.com
info@oroeditions.com

Published by ORO Editions

Preface by Curtis J. Moody
Book Design by Paul Werth Associates
Edited by Paul Werth Associates
Managing Editor: Jake Anderson

10 9 8 7 6 5 4 3 2 1 First Edition

ISBN: 978-1-943532-26-1

Color Separations and Printing: ORO Group Ltd.
Printed in China.

ORO Editions makes a continuous effort to minimize the overall carbon footprint of its publications. As part of this goal, ORO Editions, in association with Global ReLeaf, arranges to plant trees to replace those used in the manufacturing of the paper produced for its books. Global ReLeaf is an international campaign run by American Forests, one of the world's oldest nonprofit conservation organizations. Global ReLeaf is American Forests' education and action program that helps individuals, organizations, agencies, and corporations improve the local and global environment by planting and caring for trees.

MOODY NOLAN

DESIGN

VOLUME 2

TABLE OF CONTENTS

MOODY NOLAN DESIGN

PREFACE

by Curtis J. Moody
FAIA, NOMA, NCARB, LEED AP

Moody Nolan has come a long way since we laid the foundation for this company in 1982 with just two employees. Since then, we've grown from a Midwestern architecture firm to a national practice with a footprint of successes that speak to, and reflect the cultures of, our communities. Along the way we've remained true to our creative process and committed to our guiding principles.

In many respects, a lot has changed with regard to our craft. What we build and how we build it continues to grow and evolve, keeping us on our toes and always looking ahead at what's next. But at the same time, some things remain unchanged – namely why we do what we do and the principles that guide us in our work, no matter how big or small the project.

As we've grown in size and reputation, and as we've expanded nationwide into new markets, we've challenged ourselves to bridge the divides between architecture and engineering, art and science, between what is possible and what is purposeful. In fact, striking this kind of balance is among the most intriguing parts of our work. It is this sense of intrigue that has allowed us to offer solutions that perform, inspire and ultimately endure.

Our successes did not happen without exceptional talent, which is represented in this latest volume of our firm's work. The architecture represented here spans the years between 2013 and 2019 and reflects the completed projects and conceptual ideas of a firm committed to excellence with a purpose.

However, this volume is much more than an architecture book. It is also a testament to the good things that happen when clients, communities and design architects walk hand-in-hand for a common purpose.

BODY OF WORK
COMPLETED

MOODY NOLAN DESIGN

Moody Nolan's work is built on a philosophy of responsive architecture in which we begin each challenge by focusing on one central consideration: the needs of the client and the community served.

In responsive architecture, creative thought derives not only from the client's vision, but also from considering who will use the building, how they will use it and their cultural frames of reference. This way of thinking relies on intent listening, deep analysis and solutions that are simultaneously innovative, functional and beautiful.

The following pages represent our favorite environments built during the past six years, and they are examples of what we view as responsive architecture at its best.

Connor Group
Headquarters

Client Name: The Connor Group

Project Size: 39,000 sq. ft.

Cost: Confidential

Location: Miamisburg, Ohio

Role: Design Architect/Architect of Record – Moody Nolan

Awards: Honor Award, National Organization of Minority
Architects. 2016

Honor Award, American Institute of Architects,
Ohio Chapter. 2015

Merit Award, American Institute of Architects,
Columbus Chapter. 2015

New Walls Category, Metal Construction New
Building. 2015

New Construction Under $20 Million, Associated
General Contractors of Ohio. 2014

American Architecture Award, The European Centre
for Architecture Art Design and Urban Studies and
the Chicago Athenaeum. 2012

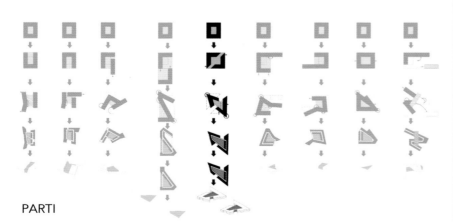

PARTI

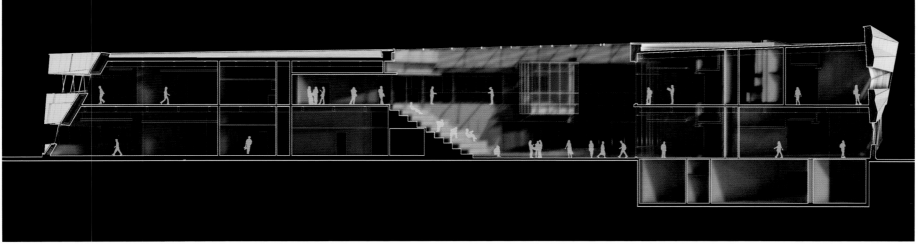

Connor Hangar

Client Name: The Connor Group

Project Size: 17,000 sq. ft.

Cost: Confidential

Location: Miamisburg, Ohio

Role: Design Architect/Architect of Record –
Moody Nolan

Awards: Honor Award, The American Institute of
Architects, Columbus Chapter. 2018

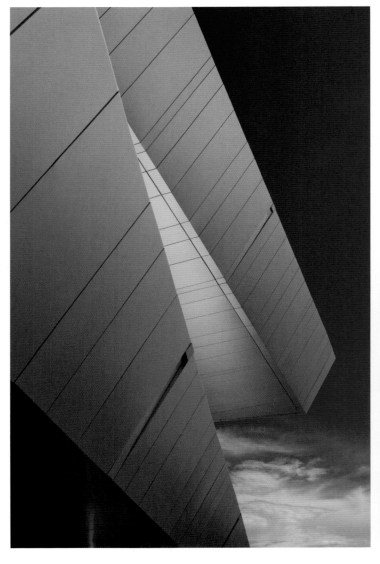

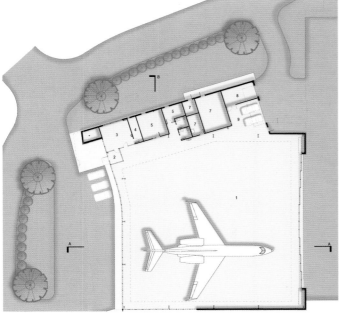

AC Hotel Columbus Dublin

Client Name: Marriott International, Inc.

Project Size: 104,000 sq. ft.

Cost: $24,000,000

Location: Dublin, Ohio

Role: Design Architect/Architect of Record – Moody Nolan

Bridge Park Mixed-Use Development

Client Name: Crawford Hoying

Project Size: 2,500,000 sq. ft.

Cost: $300,000,000

Location: Dublin, Ohio

Role: Design Architect/Architect of Record – Moody Nolan

James Cancer Hospital & Solove Research Institute

Client Name: The Ohio State University Wexner Medical Center

Project Size: 1,080,000 sq. ft.

Cost: $499,000,000

Location: Columbus, Ohio

Role: Associate Architect – Moody Nolan
      Design Architect/Architect of Record – HOK

LEED Certification: Gold

Reeb Avenue Center Renovation and Addition

Client Name: City of Columbus

Project Size: 51,894 sq. ft. Renovation and 15,658 sq. ft. Addition

Cost: $12,100,000

Location: Columbus, Ohio

Role: Design Architect/Architect of Record – Moody Nolan

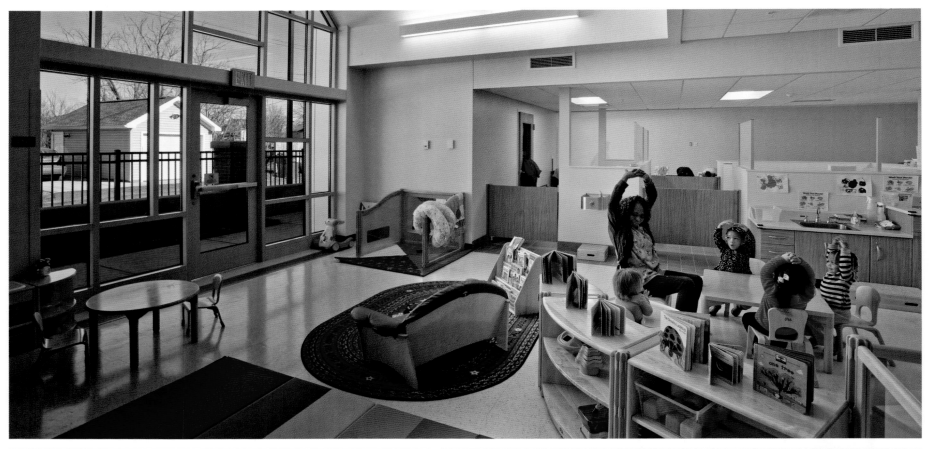

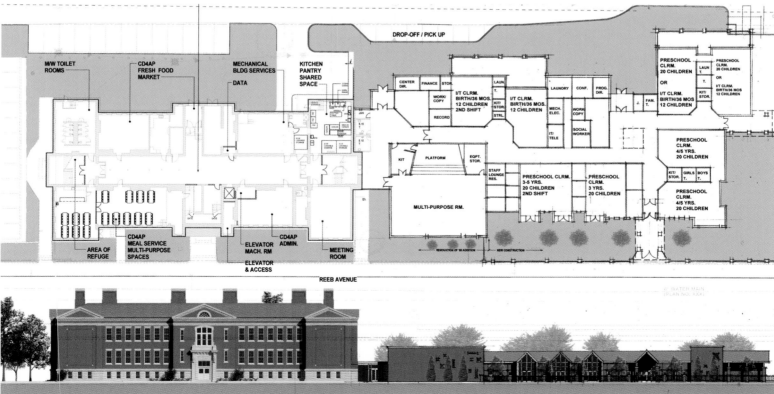

The Cal Turner Center for Student Education

Client Name: Meharry Medical College

Project Size: 80,000 sq. ft.

Cost: $24,000,000

Location: Nashville, Tennessee

Role: Design Architect/Architect of Record – Moody Nolan

LEED Certification: Certified

Awards: Middle Tennessee, Merit Award, American Institute of Architects. 2016

Design Citation, National Organization of Minority Architects. 2015

General Contractor New Construction Project, Associated General Contractors of Tennessee, Middle Tennessee. 2015

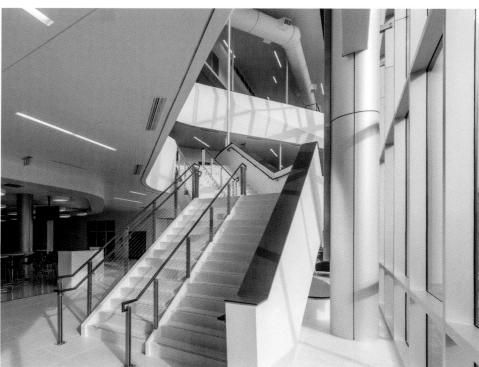

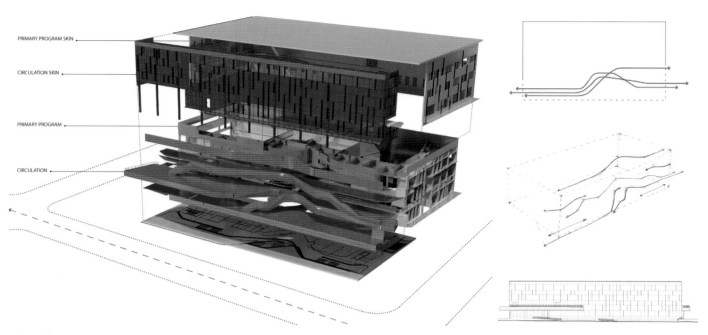

PRIMARY PROGRAM SKIN

CIRCULATION SKIN

PRIMARY PROGRAM

CIRCULATION

Circulation

The atrium is joined by a circulation system that allows all who experience the building to see the engagement happening within.

New Residence Hall

Client Name: Alabama A&M University

Project Size: 183,095 sq. ft.

Cost: $30,000,000

Location: Huntsville, Alabama

Role: Architect of Record – Moody Nolan
    Associate Architect – Chasm Architecture

Poindexter Place and Poindexter Village

Client Name: Columbus Metropolitan Housing Authority

Project Size: 101,000 sq. ft.

Cost: $13,500,000

Location: Columbus, Ohio

Role: Architect of Record – Moody Nolan
 Design Concept Consultant – City Architecture

Original Master Plan

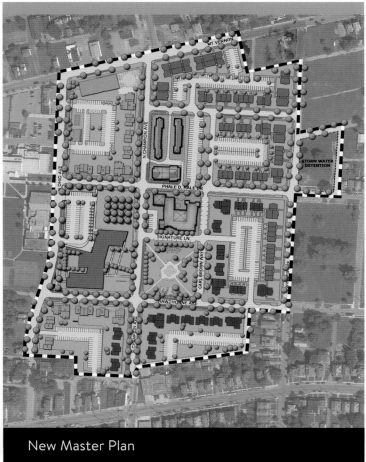

New Master Plan

New Albany Schools 2-8 Learning Community

Client Name: New Albany-Plain Local School District

Project Size: 150,000 sq. ft.

Cost: $45,000,000

Location: New Albany, Ohio

Role: Design Architect/Architect of Record – Moody Nolan

Award: Outstanding Project, Learning By Design. 2016

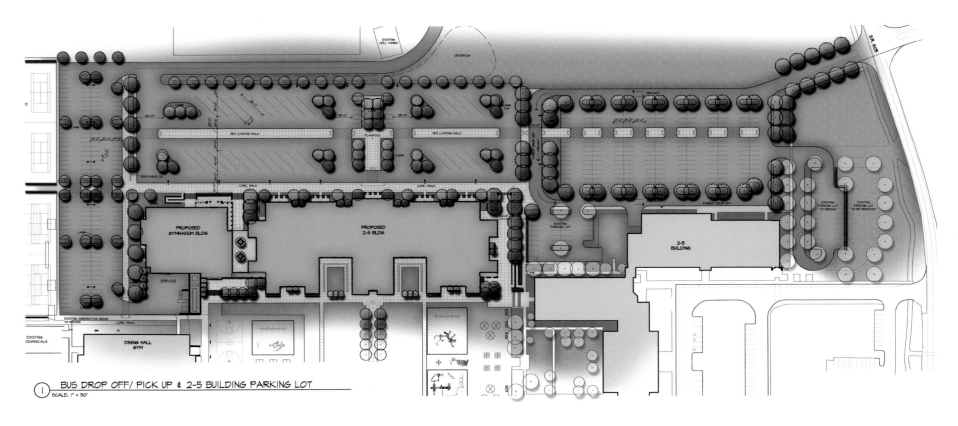

① BUS DROP OFF/ PICK UP & 2-5 BUILDING PARKING LOT
SCALE: 1" = 50'

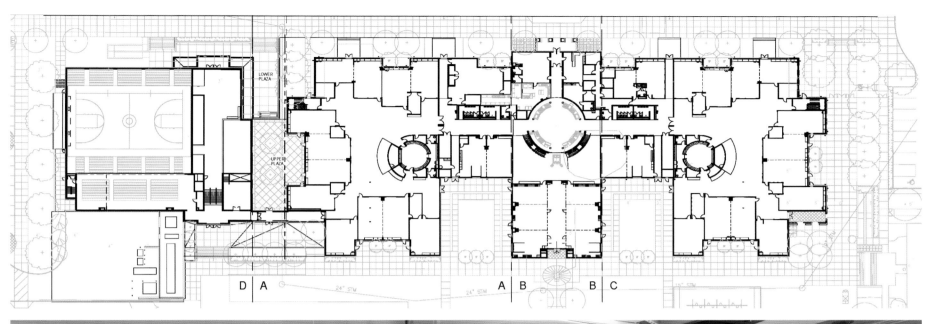

Paul Laurence Dunbar Senior High School

Client Name: D.C. Department of General Services

Project Size: 260,000 sq. ft.

Cost: $100,000,000

Location: Washington, D.C.

Role: Co-Design Architects – Moody Nolan & Perkins Eastman
    (formerly Ehrenkrantz, ECKStut & Kuhn Architects-Engineers)

LEED Certification: Platinum

Awards: Design Citation, National Organization of Minority
    Architects. 2016

    Presidential Citation in Sustainable Design, American
    Institute of Architects, D.C. Chapter. 2014

    Charter Awards: Best Civic New Building, Congress for
    New Urbanism. 2014

    Gold Citation, American School & University, Education
    Interiors Showcase. 2014

    Vision Award, Committee of 100 on the Federal City. 2014

    Honorable Mention, School Planning & Management. 2014

    Project of Distinction, Council of Educational Facility
    Planners, NE Regional Award. 2014

    Grand Prize, Learning By Design. 2013

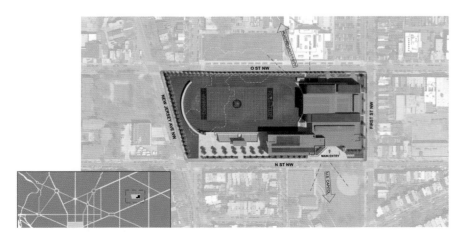

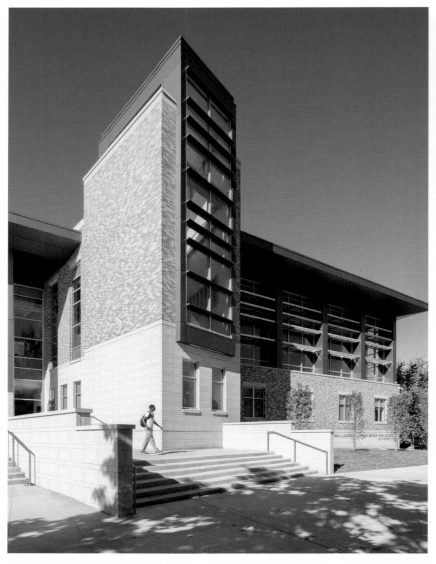

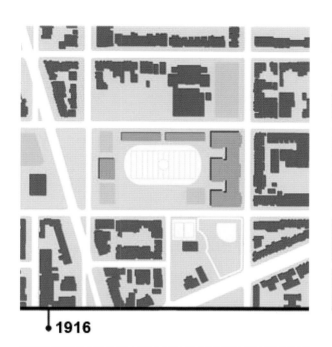

1916

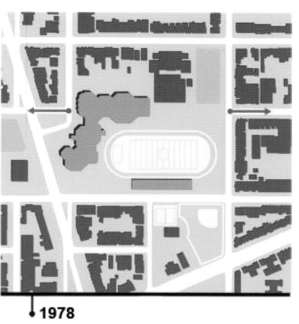

1978

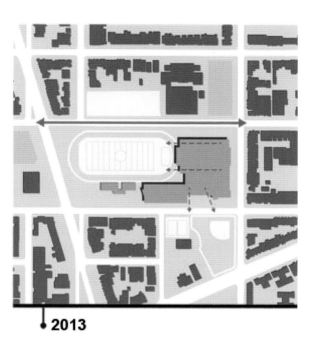

2013

Philip Heit Center for Healthy New Albany

Client Name: City of New Albany

Project Size: 55,000 sq. ft.

Cost: $10,000,000

Location: New Albany, Ohio

Role: Design Architect/Architect of Record – Moody Nolan

Arts and Sciences Building

Client Name: Indiana University Northwest/Ivy Tech
         Community College

Project Size: 133,000 sq. ft.

Cost: $45,000,000

Location: Gary, Indiana

Role: Design Architect/Architect of Record – Moody Nolan

LEED Certification: Silver

Awards: Outstanding Project Award, Learning By Design. 2018

         Outstanding Design: Post Secondary, American School
         and University. 2018

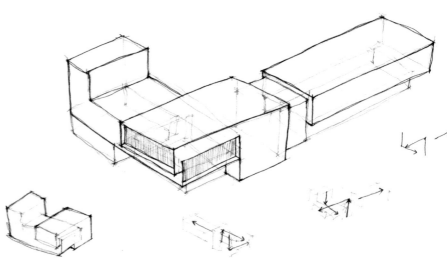

Honda Center of Excellence

Client Name: Honda of America Mfg., Inc.

Project Size: 122,000 sq. ft.

Cost: $35,000,000

Location: Marysville, Ohio

Role: Design Architect/Architect of Record – Moody Nolan

U3-X

"Pursue
your own

DREAMS.

The company
is only a tool to
accomplish them."

Soichiro Honda

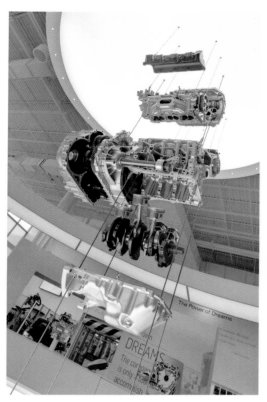

Acura MDX Body Structure

American Electric Power Transmission Building

Client Name: American Electric Power

Project Size: 195,000 sq. ft.

Cost: Confidential

Location: New Albany, Ohio

Role: Design Architect/Architect of Record – Moody Nolan

Heartland Bank Corporate Headquarters

Client Name: Heartland Bank

Project Size: 60,000 sq. ft.

Cost: $10,000,000

Location: Whitehall, Ohio

Role: Design Architect/Architect of Record – Moody Nolan

Joe and Rosie Ruhl Student Community Center

Client Name: Penn State University

Project Size: 35,000 sq. ft. Renovation and 46,000 sq. ft. Addition

Cost: $13,500,000

Location: York, Pennsylvania

Role: Design Architect – Moody Nolan
      Architect of Record – Renaissance 3 Architects

Marriott Marquis Hotel

Client Name: Metropolitan Pier and Exposition Authority

Project Size: 1,282,560 sq. ft.

Cost: $350,000,000

Location: Chicago, Illinois

Role: Associate Architect teamed with Goettsch Partners

LEED Certification: Silver

MOODY NOLAN DESIGN

STEAM Innovation Center

Client Name: Otterbein University

Project Size: 61,000 sq. ft.

Cost: $10,800,000

Location: Westerville, Ohio

Role: Design Architect/Architect of Record – Moody Nolan

OhioHealth Newborn Intensive Care Unit Expansion

Client Name: OhioHealth and Nationwide Children's Hospital

Project Size: 20,757 sq. ft.

Cost: $7,600,000

Location: Columbus, Ohio

Role: Design Architect/Architect of Record – Moody Nolan

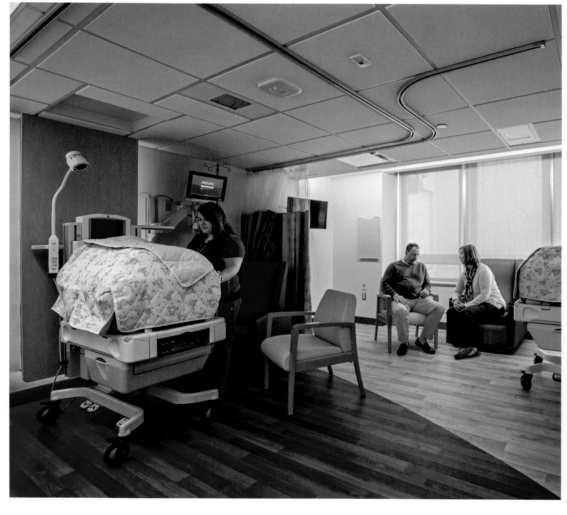

Ron J. Anderson, MD Clinic Building and Mike A. Myers Sky Bridge

Client Name: Parkland Health and Hospital System

Project Size: 245,000 sq. ft.

Cost: $54,000,000

Location: Dallas, Texas

Role: Design Architect – Moody Nolan
      Architect of Record – VAI Architects

Awards: Top Ten Award, Topping Out Awards. 2016

    M/WBE Community Impact Award, Topping Out Awards. 2016

    Outstanding Construction Award, The Associated General
    Contractors of America. 2015

MOODY NOLAN DESIGN

Mile Square Health Center

Client Name: University of Illinois at Chicago

Project Size: 121,750 sq. ft.

Cost: $42,000,000

Location: Chicago, Illinois

Role: Design Architect/Architect of Record – Moody Nolan

LEED Certification: Gold

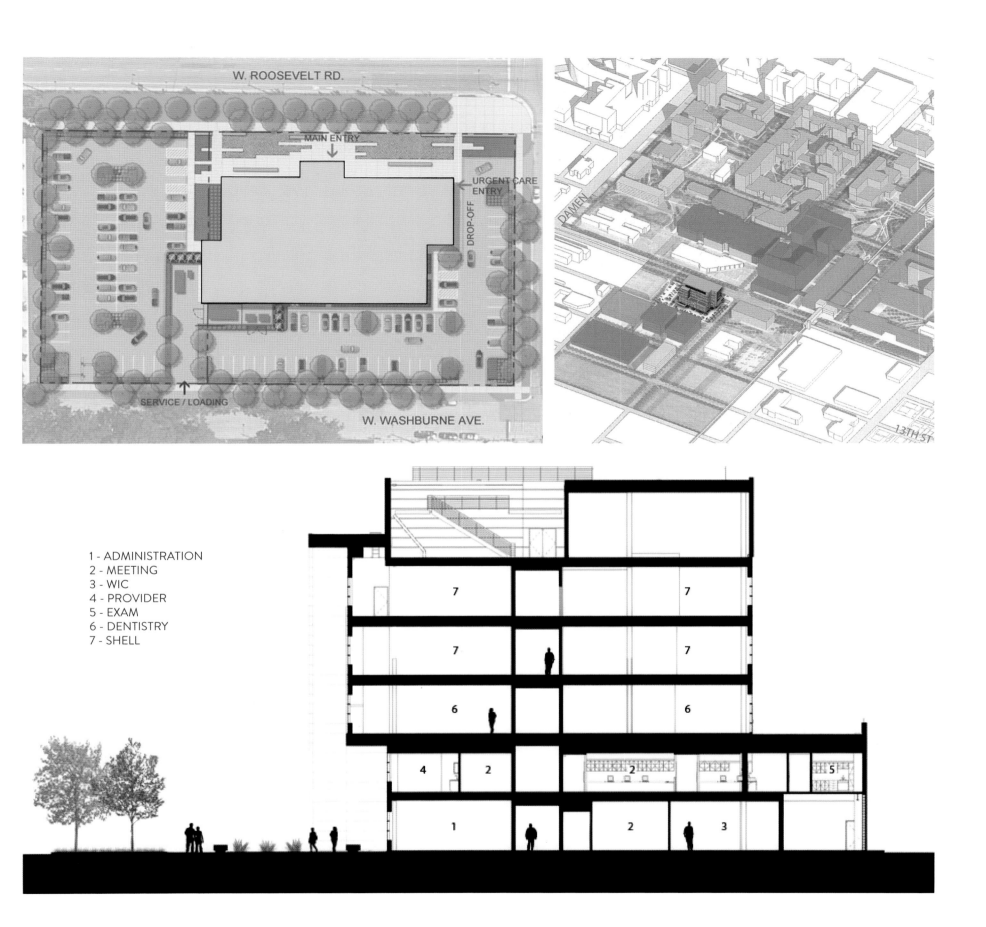

1 - ADMINISTRATION
2 - MEETING
3 - WIC
4 - PROVIDER
5 - EXAM
6 - DENTISTRY
7 - SHELL

Aramark Student Training and Recreation Complex

Client Name: Temple University

Project Size: 94,455 sq. ft.

Cost: $27,000,000

Location: Philadelphia, Pennsylvania

Role: Design Architect/Architect of Record – Moody Nolan

Award: Outstanding Engineering Achievement Award, Pennsylvania
      Society of Professional Engineers. 2017

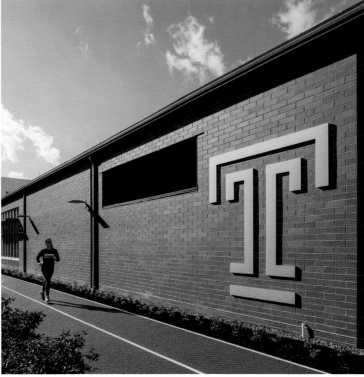

Columbus Metropolitan Library – Shepard Branch

Client Name: Columbus Metropolitan Library

Project Size: 10,000 sq. ft.

Cost: $3,850,000

Location: Columbus, Ohio

Role: Design Architect/Architect of Record – Moody Nolan

Awards: Honor Award, American Institute of Architects, Ohio Chapter.
2018

Merit Award, American Institute of Architects, Columbus Chapter.
2017

MOODY NOLAN DESIGN

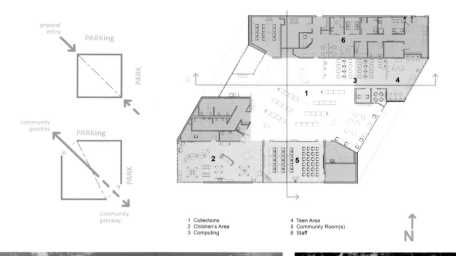

physical entry

PARKing

PARK

community porches

PARKing

PARK

community gateway

1 Collections
2 Children's Area
3 Computing
4 Teen Area
5 Community Room(s)
6 Staff

N

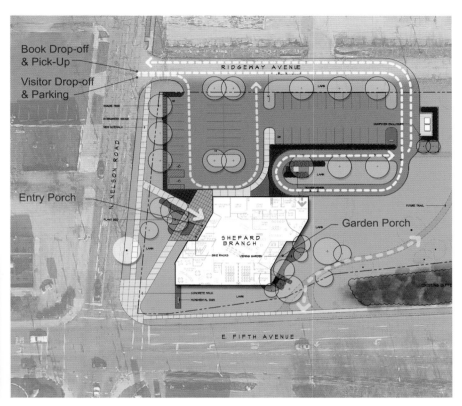

Book Drop-off & Pick-Up

Visitor Drop-off & Parking

Entry Porch

Garden Porch

RIDGEWAY AVENUE

N. NELSON ROAD

SHEPARD BRANCH

E. FIFTH AVENUE

Columbus Metropolitan Library – Parsons Branch

Client Name: Columbus Metropolitan Library

Project Size: 18,640 sq. ft.

Cost: $5,850,000

Location: Columbus, Ohio

Role: Design Architect/Architect of Record – Moody Nolan

Award: Design Citation, National Organization of Minority Architects. 2017

MOODY NOLAN DESIGN

Harvey Public Library

Client Name: Harvey Public Library District

Project Size: 22,500 sq. ft.

Cost: $6,000,000

Location: Harvey, Illinois

Role: Design Architect/Architect of Record – Moody Nolan

YMCA of Greater Cleveland

Client Name: YMCA of Greater Cleveland

Project Size: 39,000 sq. ft.

Cost: $7,800,000

Location: Cleveland, Ohio

Role: Design Architect/Architect of Record –
Moody Nolan

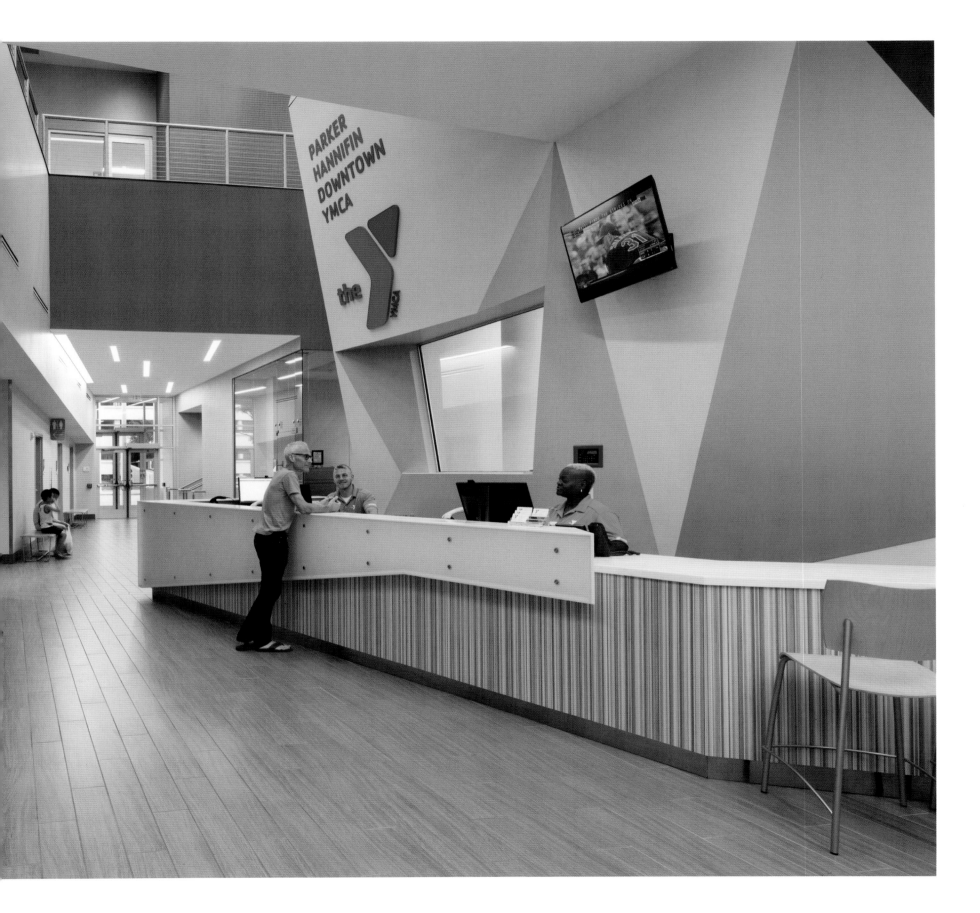

Driving Park Community Center and Pool Improvements

Client Name: City of Columbus

Project Size: 13,500 sq. ft. Renovation and 19,000 sq. ft. Addition

Cost: $10,500,000

Location: Columbus, Ohio

Role: Design Architect/Architect of Record – Moody Nolan

Before Renovation

Intramural Building

Client Name: Penn State University

Project Size: 117,039 sq. ft. Renovation and 258,000 sq. ft. Addition

Cost: $84,200,000

Location: University Park, Pennsylvania

Role: Design Architect/Architect of Record – Moody Nolan
　　　Associate Architect – APArchitects

LEED Certification: Silver

Awards: Facility of Merit, Athletic Business. 2018

　　　Outstanding Indoor Sports Facilities, National Intramural
　　　Recreation Sports Association. 2018

　　　Honorable Mention Award, Learning by Design. 2015

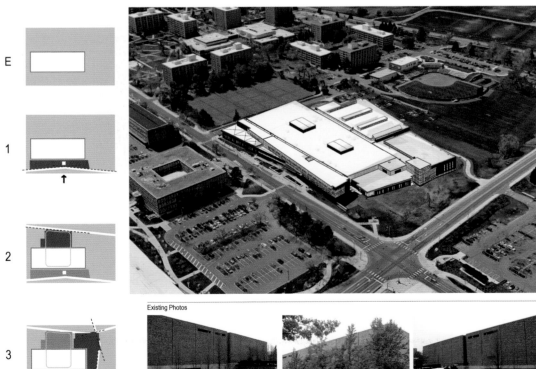

Existing Photos

Rowan College at Burlington County Student Success Center

Client Name: Rowan College at Burlington County

Project Size: 75,000 sq. ft.

Cost: $22,500,000

Location: Mount Laurel, New Jersey

Role: Design Architect – Moody Nolan
Architect of Record – USA Architects

1. Student Focused: Space designed with students mind, enhancing their educational experience.

2. Welcoming & Accessible: Comfortable, inviting, connected, transparent and logically configured space.

3. Contextual and Modern, yet Timeless: Sensitive to existing campus aesthetic, yet dynamic and appealing to students.

4. Fun, Exciting & Adaptable: Technology-rich space that creates intimate, engaging small group settings while also being able to reconfigure into larger, dynamic social spaces.

5. Unification of Campus: Destination building that is the heart of campus activities and pride.

CLIMATIC INFLUENCES

PRIMARY ENTRY VIEW

CAMPUS BOUNDARIES

CAMPUS ENTRY SEQUENCE

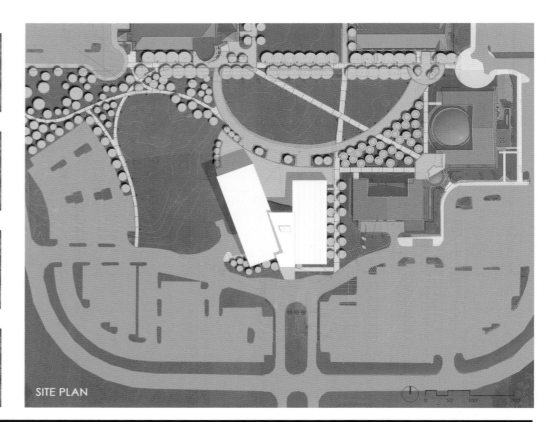

SITE PLAN

Prairie View A&M University Student Recreation Center

Client Name: Prairie View A&M University

Project Size: 92,000 sq. ft.

Cost: $24,000,000

Location: Prairie View, Texas

Role: Design Architect/Architect of Record –
    Moody Nolan
    Associate Architect – Smith Associates

Award: Excellence Award for an Education Facility,
    Associated Masonry Contractors of Houston.
    2015

MOODY NOLAN DESIGN

College of Business & Public Management

Client Name: West Chester University of Pennsylvania

Project Size: 90,000 sq. ft.

Cost: $30,000,000

Location: West Chester, Pennsylvania

Role: Design Architect – Moody Nolan
        Architect of Record – Spiezle Architectural Group

LEED Certification: Gold

Fort Nashborough Interpretive Center

Client Name: Metropolitan Board of Parks and Recreation

Project Size: 2,940 sq. ft.

Cost: $1,200,000

Location: Nashville, Tennessee

Role: Architect of Record – Moody Nolan
Interpretive Design – Encore Interpretive Design

Awards: Best New Construction Under $2M, The
Associated General Contractors of Tennessee,
Middle Tennessee Branch. 2018

Honor Award, American Institute of Architects,
Middle Tennessee. 2017

Dulles South Multipurpose Center Phase 2

Client Name: Loudoun County Parks, Recreation and Community Services

Project Size: 67,400 sq. ft.

Cost: $25,000,000

Location: South Riding, Virginia

Role: Design Architect – Moody Nolan
Architect of Record – HGA

Health and Wellness Center

Client Name: Lincoln University

Project Size: 105,000 sq. ft.

Cost: $28,000,000

Location: Lincoln University, Pennsylvania

Role: Design Architect – Moody Nolan
    Architect of Record – Renaissance 3 Architects

Award: Outstanding Design, American School &
    University, Educational Interiors Showcase. 2013

University Center

Client Name: Central State University

Project Size: 90,000 sq. ft.

Cost: $24,000,000

Location: Wilberforce, Ohio

Role: Design Architect/Architect of Record –
Moody Nolan

LEED Certification: Silver

CenturyLink Technology Center of Excellence

Client Name: CenturyLink

Project Size: 300,000 sq. ft.

Cost: $100,000,000

Location: Monroe, Louisiana

Role: Design Architect/Architect of Record –
Moody Nolan

LEED Certification: Silver

Awards: Merit Award, Illuminating Engineering
Society Design Awards. 2016.

Design Citation, National Organization
of Minority Architects. 2016

MOODY NOLAN DESIGN

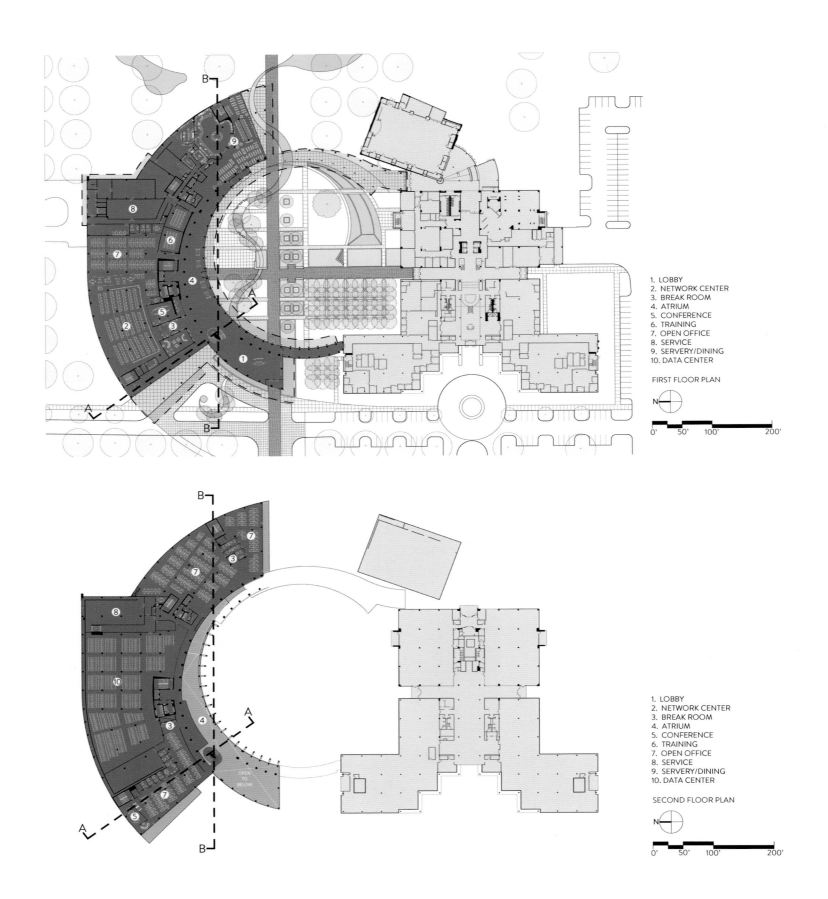

1. LOBBY
2. NETWORK CENTER
3. BREAK ROOM
4. ATRIUM
5. CONFERENCE
6. TRAINING
7. OPEN OFFICE
8. SERVICE
9. SERVERY/DINING
10. DATA CENTER

FIRST FLOOR PLAN

N

0'   50'   100'   200'

1. LOBBY
2. NETWORK CENTER
3. BREAK ROOM
4. ATRIUM
5. CONFERENCE
6. TRAINING
7. OPEN OFFICE
8. SERVICE
9. SERVERY/DINING
10. DATA CENTER

SECOND FLOOR PLAN

N

0'   50'   100'   200'

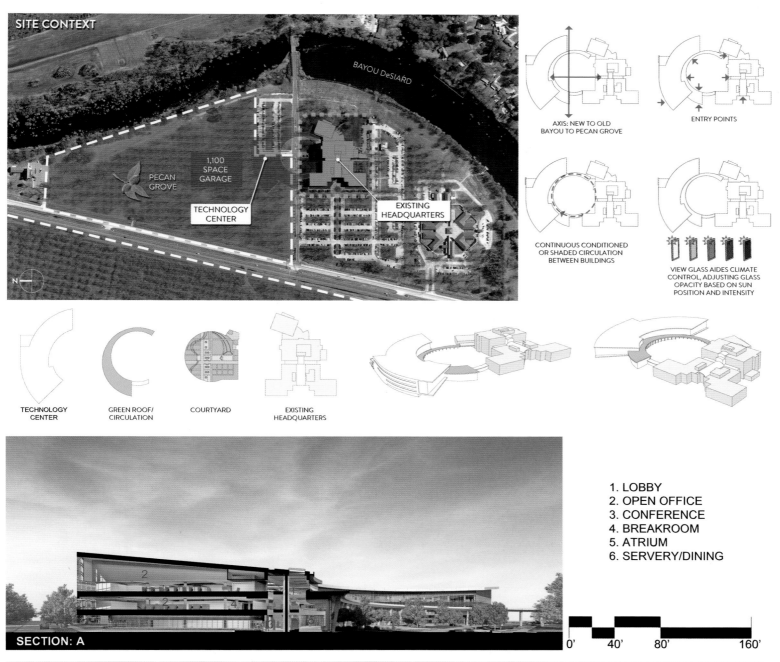

SITE CONTEXT

BAYOU DeSIARD

PECAN GROVE

1,100 SPACE GARAGE

TECHNOLOGY CENTER

EXISTING HEADQUARTERS

N

AXIS: NEW TO OLD BAYOU TO PECAN GROVE

ENTRY POINTS

CONTINUOUS CONDITIONED OR SHADED CIRCULATION BETWEEN BUILDINGS

VIEW GLASS AIDES CLIMATE CONTROL, ADJUSTING GLASS OPACITY BASED ON SUN POSITION AND INTENSITY

TECHNOLOGY CENTER

GREEN ROOF/ CIRCULATION

COURTYARD

EXISTING HEADQUARTERS

1. LOBBY
2. OPEN OFFICE
3. CONFERENCE
4. BREAKROOM
5. ATRIUM
6. SERVERY/DINING

SECTION: A

0'   40'   80'   160'

SECTION: B

Malcolm X College and School of Health Sciences

Client Name: City Colleges of Chicago

Project Size: 545,000 sq. ft. Main Building; 1,200 sq. ft. Parking Garage

Cost: $251,900,000

Location: Chicago, Illinois

Role: Architect of Record – Moody Nolan
    Criteria Architect – Cannon Design

LEED Certification: Gold

Awards: Louis I. Kahn Citation, American School and University. 2018

Honor Award, Illinois America Society of Landscape Architects. 2018

Honorable Mention Award, Learning By Design, Community College, New Construction/Addition, Entire School/Campus Building. 2018

Honor Award, Education Category, International Interior Design Association. 2017

MOODY NOLAN DESIGN

Student Center

Client Name: Kishwaukee College

Project Size: 76,000 sq. ft.

Cost: $25,000,000

Location: Malta, Illinois

Role: Design Architect – Moody Nolan
        Architect of Record – Demonica Kemper

LEED Certification: Gold

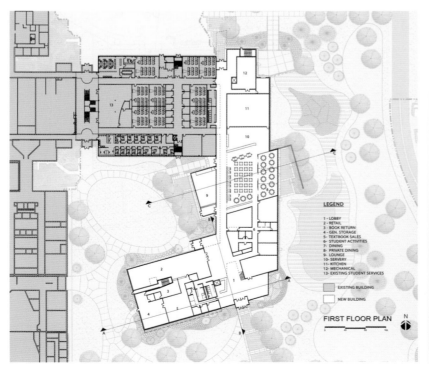

Vanderbilt University Student Recreation Center and Indoor Soccer Field

Client Name: Vanderbilt University

Project Size: 305,000 sq. ft.

Cost: $25,600,000

Location: Nashville, Tennessee

Role: Design Architect/Architect of Record – Moody Nolan

Apex Aquatics and Fitness Center

Client Name: City of McKinney

Project Size: 80,000 sq. ft.

Cost: $30,000,000

Location: McKinney, Texas

Role: Design Architect – Moody Nolan
   Architect of Record – Brinkley Sargent Architects

Awards: Recreation Facility Design Excellence Award, Texas Recreation and Park Society (TRAPS) North Region. 2017

   Best Projects Government Public Buildings Category Award of Merit, ENR Texas & Louisiana. 2017

Kempsville Recreation Center

Client Name: City of Virginia Beach
Department of Parks and Recreation

Project Size: 81,000 sq. ft.

Cost: $25,000,000

Location: Virginia Beach, Virginia

Role: Design Architect – Moody Nolan
Architect of Record – HBA

Awards: Juror's Choice Award, Hampton Roads
Association for Commercial Real Estate.
2017

Award of Excellence, Best Recreation/
Entertainment Project. 2017

MOODY NOLAN DESIGN

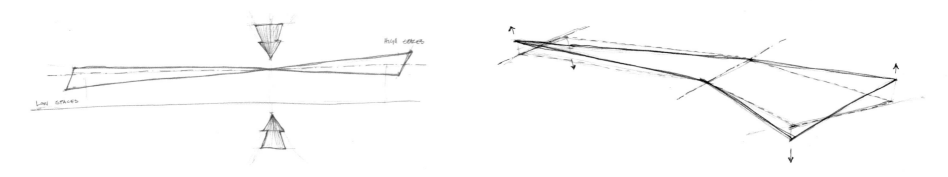

Walter Fieldhouse

Client Name: Ohio University

Project Size: 90,000 sq. ft.

Cost: $12,500,000

Location: Athens, Ohio

Role: Criteria Architect – Moody Nolan
       Architect of Record – Braun Steidl

MOODY NOLAN DESIGN

Wintrust Arena

Client Name: Metropolitan Pier & Exposition Authority (MPEA) DePaul University

Project Size: 285,000 sq. ft.

Cost: $155,000,000

Location: Chicago, Illinois

Role: Architect of Record – Moody Nolan
Design Architects – Pelli Clarke Pelli Architects

Awards: American Architectural Award, The Chicago Athenaeum: Museum of Architecture and Design and The European Centre for Architecture Art Design and Urban Studies. 2018

Platinum Award, Building Design + Construction. 2018

Illumination Award of Merit, Illuminating Engineering Society. 2018

Project of the Year - New Construction, Construction Industry Service Corporation. 2018

MOODY NOLAN DESIGN

Steinhauer-Rogan-Black Humanities Building

Client Name: Volunteer State Community College

Project Size: 86,000 sq. ft.

Cost: $27,000,000

Location: Gallatin, Tennessee

Role: Design Architect/Architect of Record – Moody Nolan

Award: Award of Merit, Associated General Contractors. 2017

Broadview Heights Health Center

Client Name: University Hospitals

Project Size: 51,000 sq. ft.

Cost: $18,000,000

Location: Broadview Heights, Ohio

Role: Design Architect/Architect of Record – Moody Nolan

LEED Certification: Silver

Integrated Education Center

Client Name: Ohio University

Project Size: 86,000 sq. ft.

Cost: $12,000,000

Location: Dublin, Ohio

Role: Design Architect/Architect of Record – Moody Nolan

St. Ann's Hospital Expansion

Client Name: Mount Carmel Health System

Project Size: 127,000 sq. ft.

Cost: $80,000,000

Location: Westerville, Ohio

Role: Design Architect/Architect of Record –
    Moody Nolan

MOODY NOLAN DESIGN

OVERALL PATIENT TOWER
FIRST FLOOR

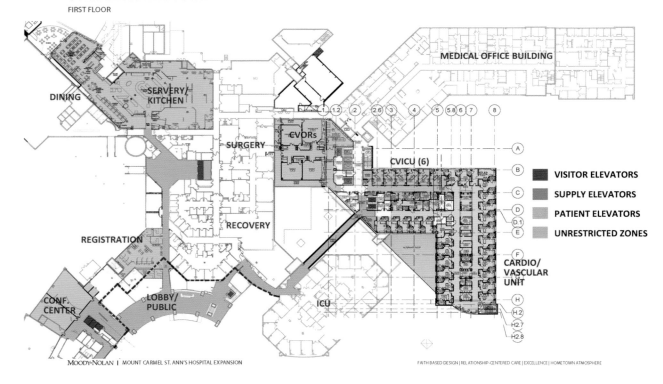

MEDICAL OFFICE BUILDING

DINING

SERVERY/
KITCHEN

SURGERY

CVORs

CVICU (6)

RECOVERY

REGISTRATION

CARDIO/
VASCULAR
UNIT

CONF.
CENTER

LOBBY/
PUBLIC

ICU

VISITOR ELEVATORS

SUPPLY ELEVATORS

PATIENT ELEVATORS

UNRESTRICTED ZONES

MOODY·NOLAN | MOUNT CARMEL ST. ANN'S HOSPITAL EXPANSION

FAITH BASED DESIGN | RELATIONSHIP-CENTERED CARE | EXCELLENCE | HOMETOWN ATMOSPHERE

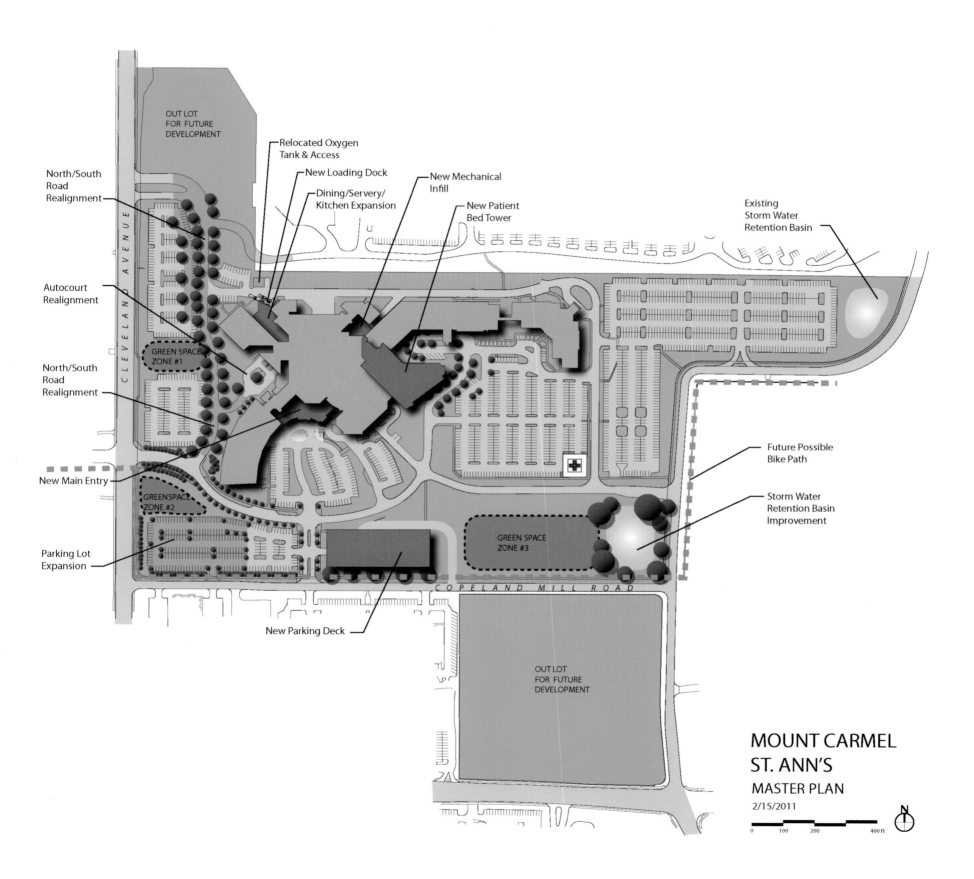

OUT LOT FOR FUTURE DEVELOPMENT

Relocated Oxygen Tank & Access

New Loading Dock

Dining/Servery/ Kitchen Expansion

New Mechanical Infill

New Patient Bed Tower

Existing Storm Water Retention Basin

North/South Road Realignment

Autocourt Realignment

GREEN SPACE ZONE #1

North/South Road Realignment

New Main Entry

GREENSPACE ZONE #2

Parking Lot Expansion

CLEVELAND AVENUE

New Parking Deck

GREEN SPACE ZONE #3

Future Possible Bike Path

Storm Water Retention Basin Improvement

COPELAND MILL ROAD

OUT LOT FOR FUTURE DEVELOPMENT

MOUNT CARMEL
ST. ANN'S
MASTER PLAN
2/15/2011

0   100   200   400 ft

France A. Córdova Recreational Sports Center Expansion and Renovation

Client Name: Purdue University

Project Size: 420,000 sq. ft.

Cost: $103,000,000

Location: West Lafayette, Indiana

Role: Design Architect/Architect of Record – Moody Nolan

LEED Certification: Gold

Awards: Honor Citation, National Organization of Minority Architects. 2015

Merit Award, American Institute of Architects, Indiana Chapter. 2015

International Architecture Award, The European Centre for Architecture Art Design and Urban Studies and the Chicago Anthenaeum. 2015

Facility Design Award, Association of College Unions International. 2015

Facility of Merit, Athletic Business. 2014

Merit Award for Newly Completed Buildings, Additions, Remodelings, Renovations, Restorations, American Institute of Architects, Ohio Chapter. 2014

Collegiate Citation, Top Post-Secondary, American School & University, Educational Interiors Showcase. 2014

Outstanding Indoor Sports Facilities, National Intramural Recreation Sports Association. 2014

Honorable Mention, Learning by Design. 2013

MOODY NOLAN DESIGN

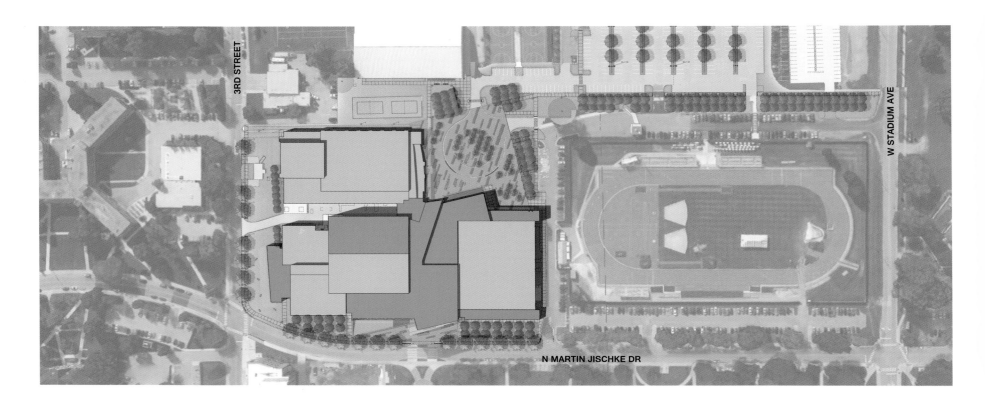

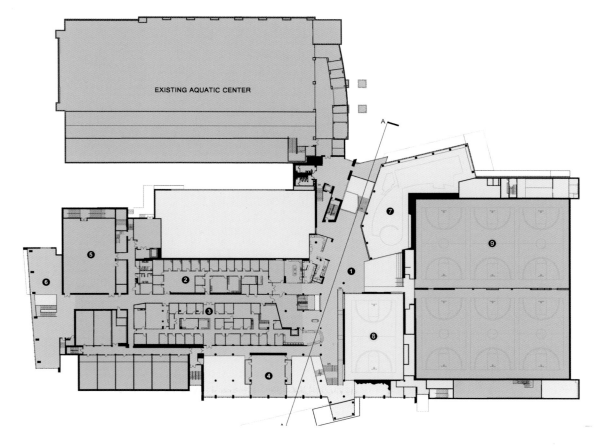

EXISTING AQUATIC CENTER

Memorial Union

Client Name: University of Wisconsin – Madison

Project Size: Phase 1 – 129,435 sq. ft.; Phase 2 – 128,960 sq. ft.

Cost: Phase 1 – $38,000,000; Phase 2 – $36,000,000

Location: Madison, Wisconsin

Role: Design Architect – Moody Nolan
      Architect of Record – Uihlein Wilson Architects

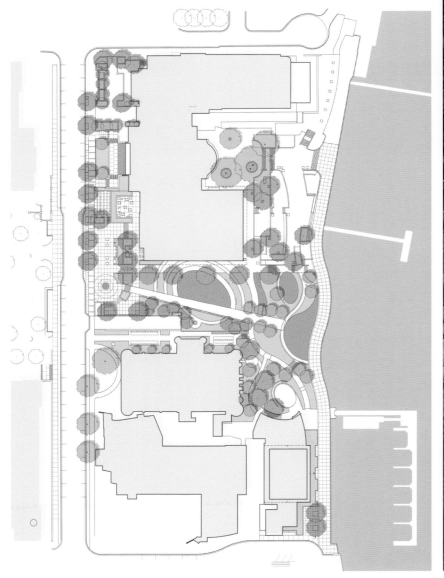

Alliance Data Office Park

Client Name: The Georgetown Company

Project Size: 570,000 sq. ft.

Cost: $80,000,000

Location: Columbus, Ohio

Role: Design Architect/Architect of Record – Moody Nolan

MOODY NOLAN DESIGN

Cardinal Hall

Client Name: The Ohio Expo Center & State Fair

Project Size: 100,000 sq. ft.

Cost: $22,000,000

Location: Columbus, Ohio

Role: Design Architect/Architect of Record –
Moody Nolan

Beta Theta Pi Chapter House

Client Name: Theta Delta of Beta Theta Pi Alumni Association – The Ohio State University

Project Size: 24,700 sq. ft.

Cost: $5,000,000

Location: Columbus, Ohio

Role: Design Architect/Architect of Record – Moody Nolan

Donald Julian Reaves Student Activities Center

Client Name: Winston-Salem State University

Project Size: 90,000 sq. ft.

Cost: $27,400,000

Location: Winston-Salem, North Carolina

Role: Design Architect – Moody Nolan
    Architect of Record – Woolpert

LEED Certification: Gold

Awards: Outstanding Indoor Sports Facilities Award,
    National Intramural Recreation Sports Association. 2015

    Grand Prize, Learning by Design. 2014

    Excellence in Student-Centered Facilities, Association
    of College Unions International. 2014

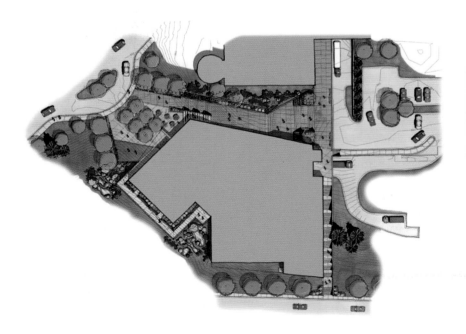

KIPP: Charter School Campus

Client Name: KIPP Columbus

Project Size: 58,000 sq. ft. Primary School/Early
Childhood Education; 140,000 sq. ft.
Elementary & Middle School;
100,400 sq. ft. High School;
600 Seat/6,000 sq. ft. Stadium

Cost: Confidential

Location: Columbus, Ohio

Role: Design Architect/Architect of Record for
Primary, Elementary and Middle School –
Moody Nolan
Architect of Record for High School –
Moody Nolan
Design Architect for High School –
Kathleen Baldwin

Award: Honor Award, American Institute of
Architects, Ohio Chapter. 2018

Independent 1-12 Day School

Client Name: Marburn Academy

Project Size: 64,000 sq. ft.

Cost: $10,500,000

Location: New Albany, Ohio

Role: Design Architect/Architect of Record – Moody Nolan

Kappa Kappa Gamma National Headquarters

Client Name: Kappa Kappa Gamma

Project Size: 22,000 sq. ft.

Cost: $1,700,000

Location: Dublin, Ohio

Role: Design Architect/Architect of Record – Moody Nolan

Cleveland School of the Arts

Client Name: Cleveland Metropolitan School District

Project Size: 126,123 sq. ft.

Cost: $42,000,000

Location: Cleveland, Ohio

Role: Design Architect/Architect of Record – Moody Nolan

LEED Certification: Silver

Awards: Awards of Excellence, Outstanding Project Specialized Education Facility, Learning By Design. 2017

Design Citation, National Organization of Minority Architects. 2017

Building the Circle Award, University Circle, Inc. 2015

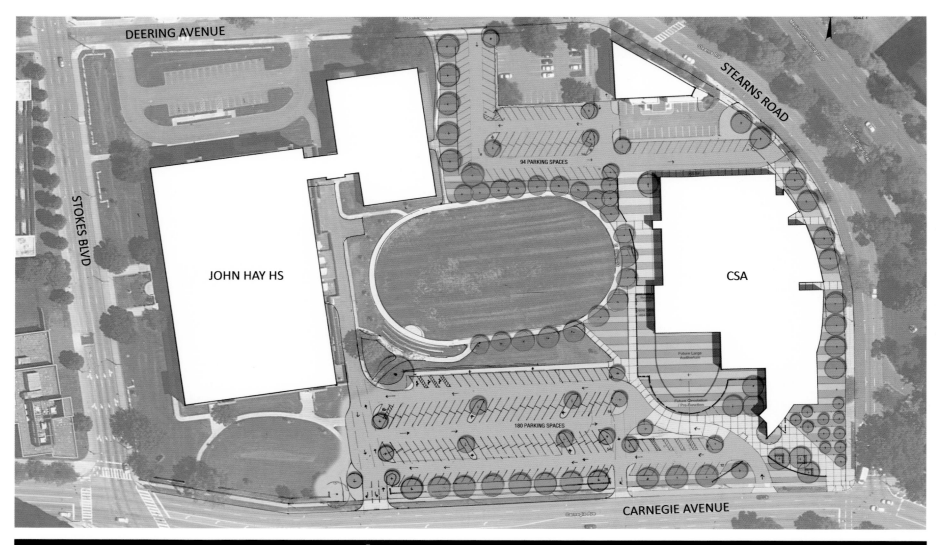

DEERING AVENUE

STEARNS ROAD

STOKES BLVD

JOHN HAY HS

CSA

94 PARKING SPACES

180 PARKING SPACES

CARNEGIE AVENUE

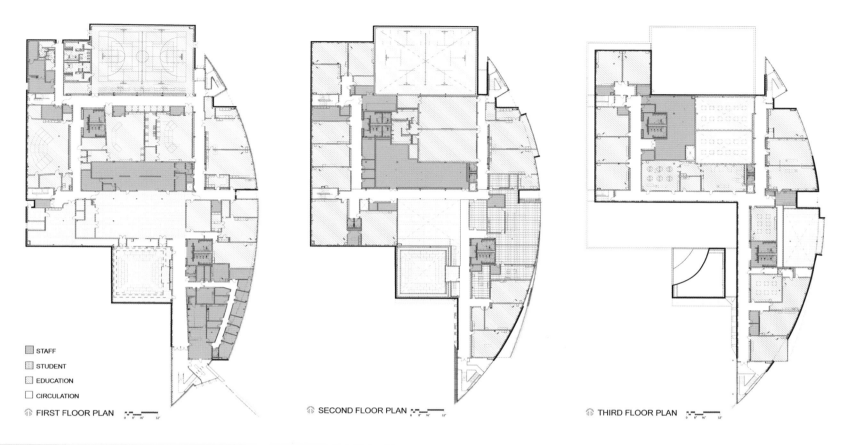

STAFF
STUDENT
EDUCATION
CIRCULATION

⇧ FIRST FLOOR PLAN

⇧ SECOND FLOOR PLAN

⇧ THIRD FLOOR PLAN

Cravath Hall

Client Name: Fisk University

Project Size: 74,000 sq. ft.

Cost: $13,700,000

Location: Nashville, Tennessee

Role: Design Architect/Architect of Record – Moody Nolan

Awards: Design Excellence, National Organization of Minority Architects. 2005

Merit Award for Historic Preservation and Renovation, American Institute of Architects, Ohio Chapter. 2005

Excellence in Design Award, Excellence in Development of Middle Tennessee. 2004

National Preservation Honor Awards, National Trust for Historic Preservation. 2004

Building Award Winner in Educational and Institutional Category, Nashville Metro Historical Commission. 2004

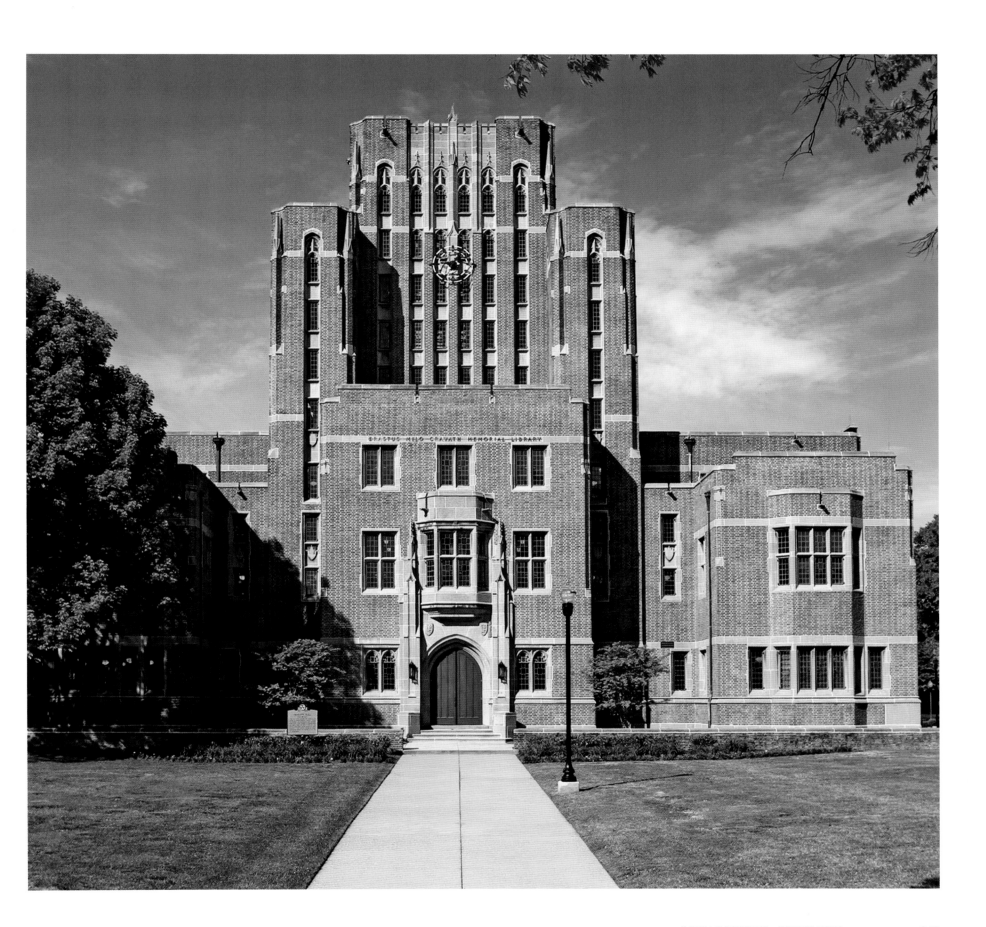

BODY OF WORK
CONCEPTUAL

MOODY NOLAN DESIGN

Moody Nolan architects relish the creative expression inherent in the iterative process. As projects move from vision to reality, design concepts become the manifestation of our total energy, creativity and thought.

Sometimes we push the boundaries of what's possible, moving the bar higher for future projects. As we envision and execute these new possibilities, some of our most cherished concepts wait to be built. We include conceptual projects here to showcase the wide-ranging creativity of Moody Nolan's architects and their approach to responsive architecture.

Library Learning Center

Client Name: Texas Southern University

Project Size: 137,000 sq. ft.

Cost: $43,000,000

Location: Houston, Texas

Role: Design Architect/Architect of Record – Moody Nolan

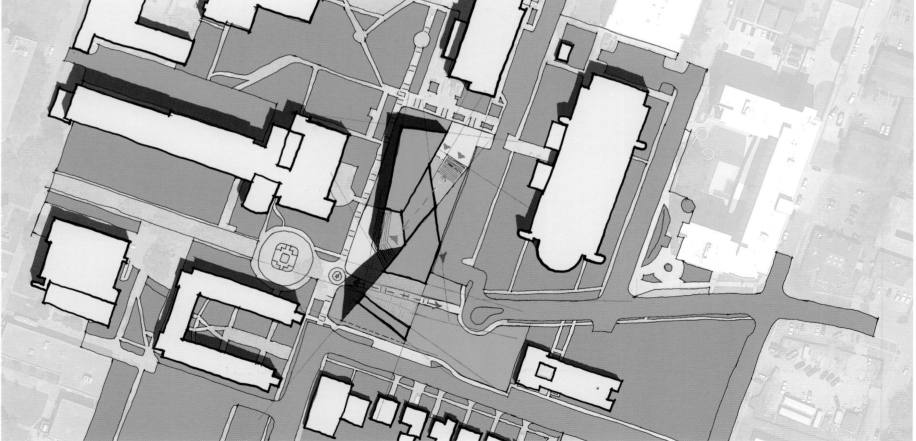

Columbus Metropolitan Library – Martin Luther King Branch

Client Name: Columbus Metropolitan Library

Project Size: 18,700 sq. ft.

Cost: $5,700,000

Location: Columbus, Ohio

Role: Design Architect/Architect of Record – Moody Nolan

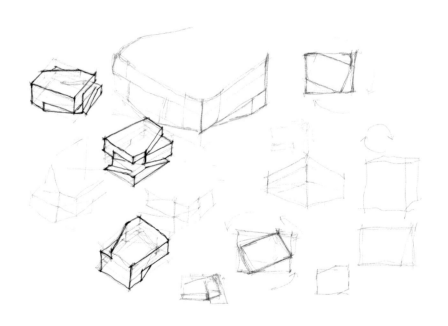

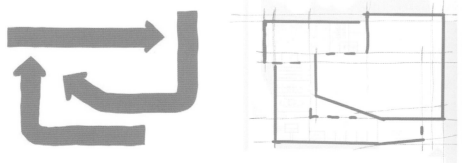

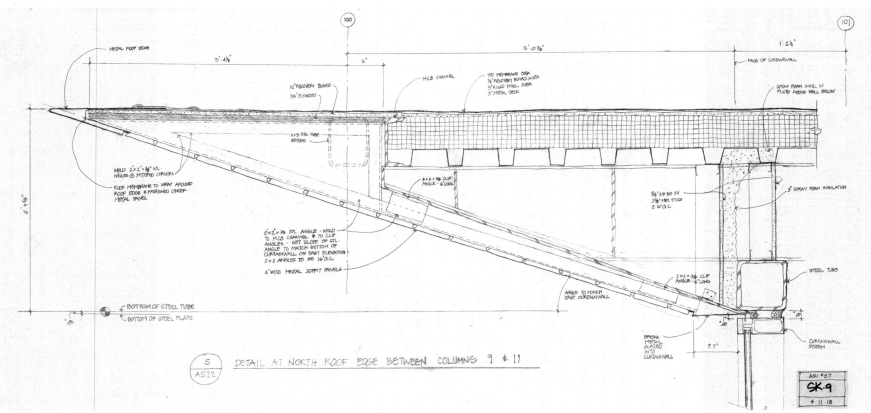

DETAIL AT NORTH ROOF EDGE BETWEEN COLUMNS 9 & 11

Cuyahoga County Public Library – Bay Village Branch

Client Name: Cuyahoga County Public Library

Project Size: 16,000 sq. ft.

Cost: $6,000,000

Location: Bay Village, Ohio

Role: Design Architect/Architect of Record – Moody Nolan

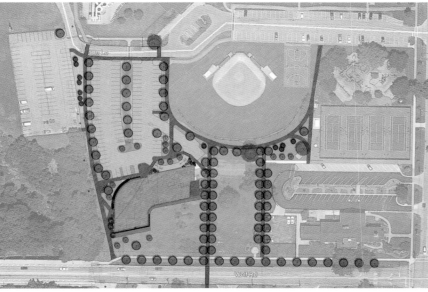

Omni Boston Hotel at the Seaport

Client Name: Massachusetts Port Authority

Project Size: 1,000,000 sq. ft.

Cost: $550,000,000

Location: Boston, Massachusetts

Role: Interior Architect – Moody Nolan
      Core and Shell Designer – Elkus Manfredi

Moxy Hotel

Client Name: Crawford Hoying

Project Size: 165,000 sq. ft.

Cost: $24,000,000

Location: Columbus, Ohio

Role: Design Architect/Architect of Record –
    Moody Nolan

Westshore Campus Phase II

Client Name: Cuyahoga Community College

Project Size: 85,000 sq. ft. Addition and 15,000 sq. ft. Renovation

Cost: $39,000,000

Location: Westlake, Ohio

Role: Design Architect/Architect of Record – Moody Nolan

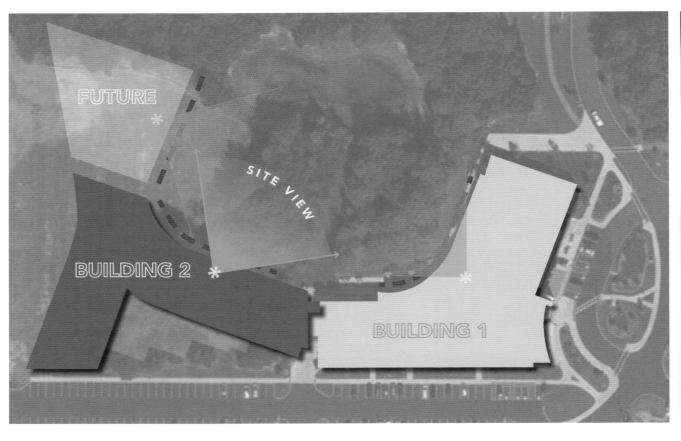

FUTURE *

SITE VIEW

BUILDING 2 *

BUILDING 1 *

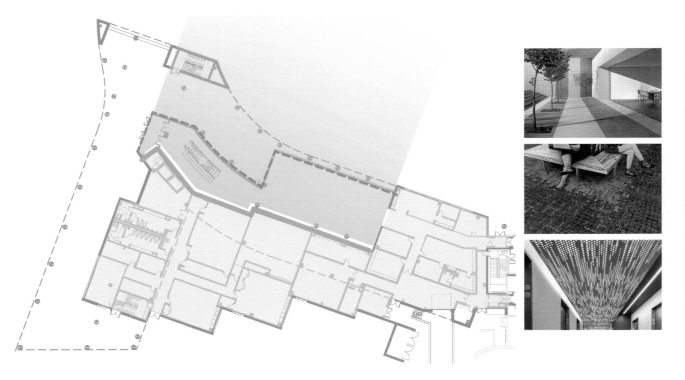

Student Success Center

Client Name: The University of North Texas at Dallas

Project Size: 131,000 sq. ft.

Cost: $48,000,000

Location: Richardson, Texas

Role: Design Architect/Architect of Record – Moody Nolan
      Associate Architect – VAI Architects

Covelli Multi-Sport Arena

Client Name: The Ohio State University

Project Size: 120,000 sq. ft.

Cost: $39,000,000

Location: Columbus, Ohio

Role: Architect of Record – Moody Nolan
       Design Architect – Populous

Panzer Stadium

Client Name: Penn State University

Cost: $6,800,000

Location: State College, Pennsylvania

Role: Design Architect/Architect of Record –
Moody Nolan
Associate Architect – APArchitects

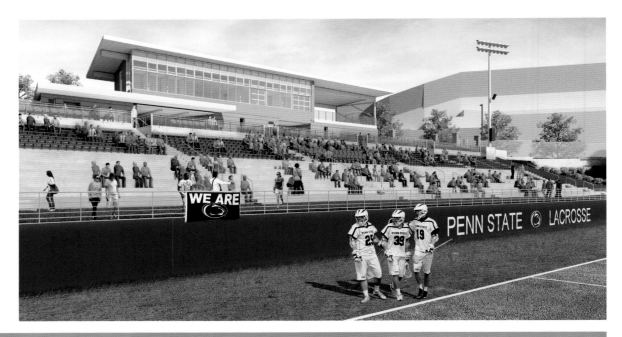

Davidson County Criminal Justice Center

Client Name: Metropolitan Government of
Nashville and Davidson County

Project Size: 260,000 sq. ft.

Cost: $110,000,000

Location: Nashville, Tennessee

Role: Associate Architect – Moody Nolan
Design Architect/Architect of Record – HOK

3750 Lancaster Development Concept

Client Name: Southern Land Company

Project Size: 260,000 sq. ft.

Cost: $39,000,000

Location: Philadelphia, Pennsylvania

Role: Design Architect – Moody Nolan
    Architect of Record – Voith & Mactavish Architects

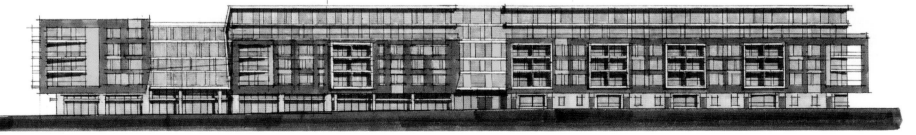

North Market Tower

Client Name: City of Columbus, Ohio

Project Size: 300,000 sq. ft.

Location: Columbus, Ohio

Role: Design Architect/Architect of Record – Moody Nolan

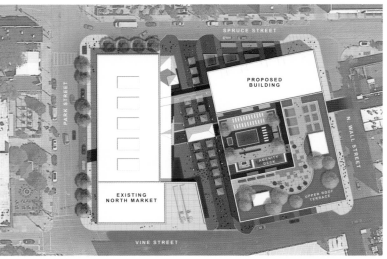

Historic District Parking Garage

Client Name: City of Dublin

Project Size: 450–500 parking spaces

Cost: $10,000,000

Location: Dublin, Ohio

Role: Design Architect/Architect of Record – Moody Nolan

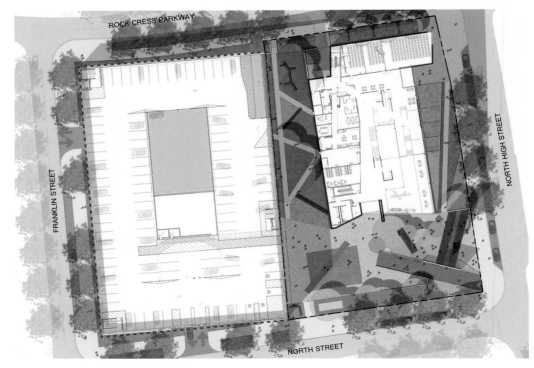

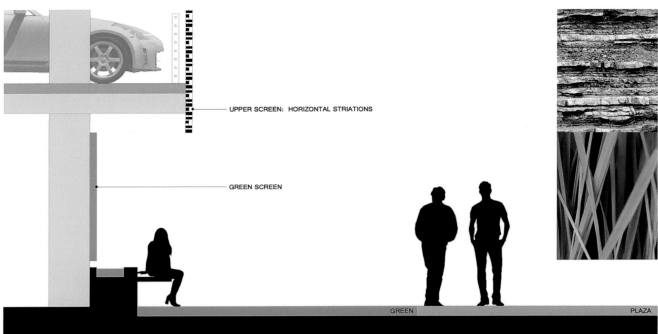

UPPER SCREEN: HORIZONTAL STRIATIONS

GREEN SCREEN

GREEN   PLAZA

Consolidated Rental Agency Center (CONRAC) at John Glenn Columbus International Airport

Client Name: Columbus Regional Airport Authority

Project Size: 3,076 parking spaces

Cost: $139,000,000

Location: Columbus, Ohio

Role: Design Architect – Moody Nolan
        Architect of Record – TranSystems

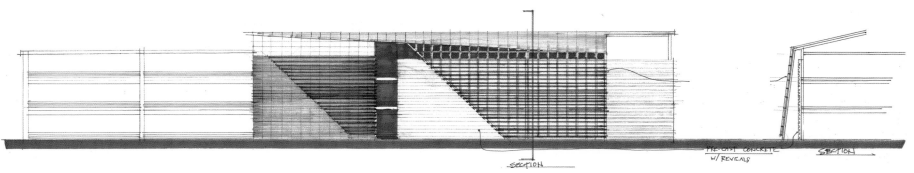

Javits Center

Client Name: Empire State Development Corporation

Project Size: 1,200,000 sq. ft.

Cost: $1,550,000,000

Location: New York City, New York

Role: Architect of Record – Truck Marshaling Facility –
 Moody Nolan
 Design Architect – tvsdesign

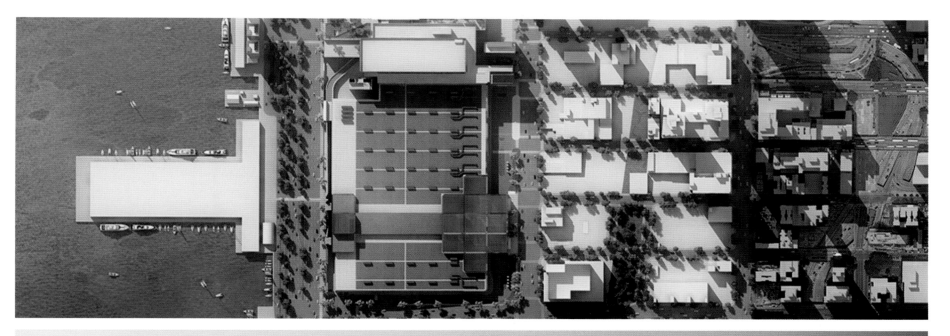

OhioHealth Administrative Office Project

Client Name: OhioHealth

Project Size: 270,000 sq. ft.

Cost: $83,000,000

Location: Columbus, Ohio

Role: Design Architect/Architect of Record – Moody Nolan

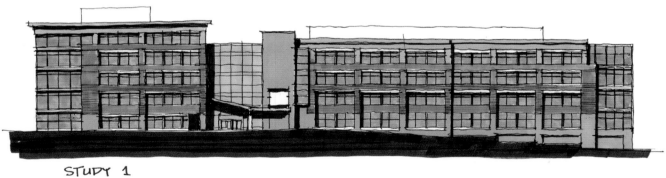

STUDY 1

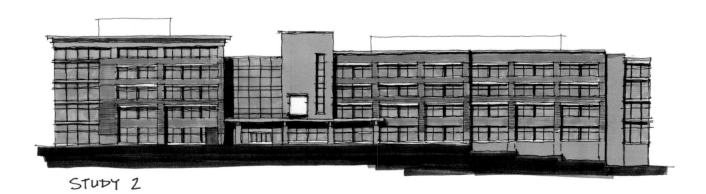

STUDY 2

Edgewood Recreation Center

Client Name: D.C. Department of General Services

Project Size: 19,400 sq. ft.

Cost: $18,000,000

Location: Washington, D.C.

Role: Design Architect/Architect of Record – Moody Nolan

Student Recreation Center

Client Name: University of Connecticut

Project Size: 200,000 sq. ft.

Cost: $75,000,000

Location: Storrs, Connecticut

Role: Co-Design Architects – Moody Nolan & JCJ Architecture

Norris University Center

Client Name: Northwestern University

Project Size: 254,000 sq. ft.

Location: Evanston, Illinois

Role: Design Architect/Architect of Record – Moody Nolan

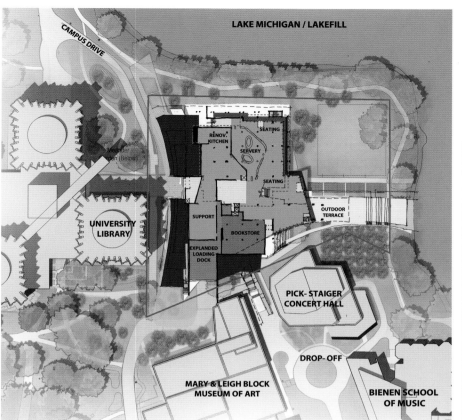

CAMPUS DRIVE

LAKE MICHIGAN / LAKEFILL

UNIVERSITY LIBRARY

Meander Garden (Below)

RENOV. KITCHEN

SEATING

SERVERY

SEATING

SUPPORT

BOOKSTORE

EXPLANDED LOADING DOCK

OUTDOOR TERRACE

PICK- STAIGER CONCERT HALL

DROP- OFF

MARY & LEIGH BLOCK MUSEUM OF ART

BIENEN SCHOOL OF MUSIC

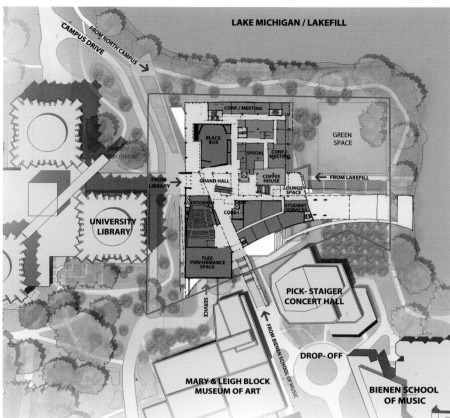

CAMPUS DRIVE

FROM NORTH CAMPUS

LAKE MICHIGAN / LAKEFILL

UNIVERSITY LIBRARY

Meander Garden (Below)

FROM LIBRARY

CONF./ MEETING

BLACK BOX

SPECIAL

CONF. MEETING

GREEN SPACE

GRAND HALL

COFFEE HOUSE

LOUNGE SPACE

FROM LAKEFILL

AUDITORIUM

CONF.

STUDENT SERVICES

FLEX PERFORMANCE SPACE

SERVICE

FROM BIENEN SCHOOL OF MUSIC

PICK- STAIGER CONCERT HALL

DROP- OFF

MARY & LEIGH BLOCK MUSEUM OF ART

BIENEN SCHOOL OF MUSIC

Student Center and Housing

Client Name: Bethune-Cookman University

Project Size: 160,000 sq. ft.

Cost: $24,000,000

Location: Daytona Beach, Florida

Role: Design Architect/Architect of Record – Moody Nolan

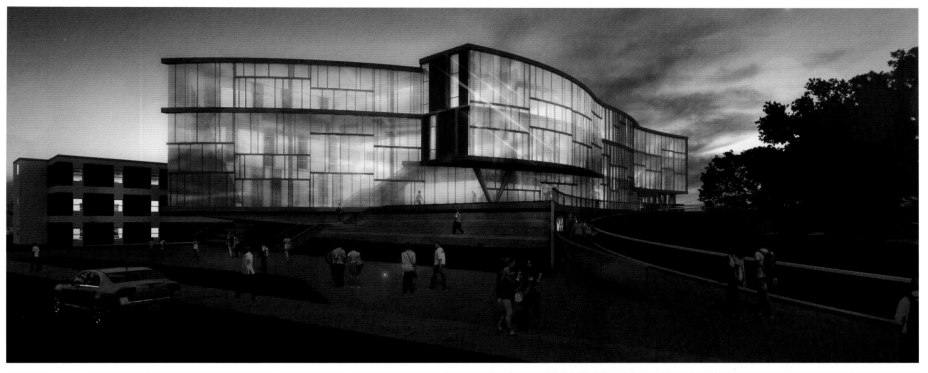

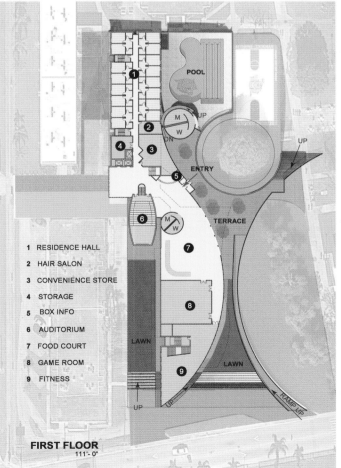

FIRST FLOOR
111'- 0"

1 RESIDENCE HALL
2 HAIR SALON
3 CONVENIENCE STORE
4 STORAGE
5 BOX INFO
6 AUDITORIUM
7 FOOD COURT
8 GAME ROOM
9 FITNESS

POOL

ENTRY

TERRACE

LAWN

LAWN

International African American Museum (IAAM)

Client Name: City of Charleston

Project Size: 41,000 sq. ft.

Cost: $75,000,000

Location: Charleston, South Carolina

Role: Architect of Record – Moody Nolan
    Design Architect – Pei Cobb Freed & Partners

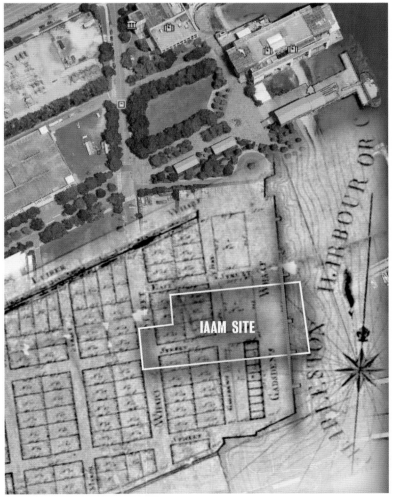

John F. Kennedy High School

Client Name: Cleveland Metropolitan School District

Project Size: 149,100 sq. ft.

Cost: $31,538,000

Location: Cleveland, Ohio

Role: Design Architect/Architect of Record – Moody Nolan

Jack Yates High School

Client Name: Houston Independent
School District

Project Size: 210,000 sq. ft.

Cost: $59,000,000

Location: Houston, Texas

Role: Design Architect/Architect of
Record – Moody Nolan

Fitness and Wellness Center

Client Name: Jacksonville State University

Project Size: 104,500 sq. ft.

Cost: $32,600,000

Location: Jacksonville, Alabama

Role: Design Architect/Architect of Record –
 Moody Nolan

South Side High School

Client Name: Chicago Public Schools

Project Size: 160,000 sq. ft.

Cost: $69,889,000

Location: Chicago, Illinois

Role: Design Architect/Architect of Record –
    Moody Nolan
    Associate Architect – Brook Architecture

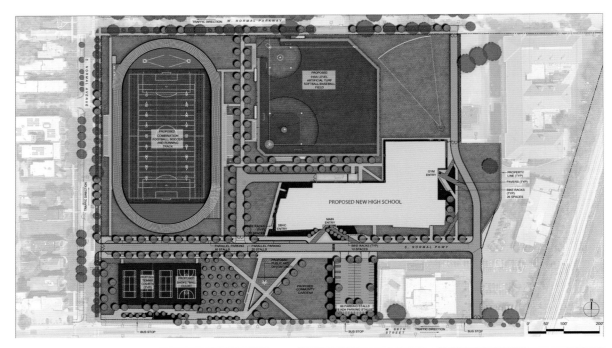

Rainbow Center for Women & Children

Client Name: University Hospitals

Project Size: 40,000 sq. ft.

Cost: $24,000,000

Location: Cleveland, Ohio

Role: Design Architect/Architect of Record – Moody Nolan

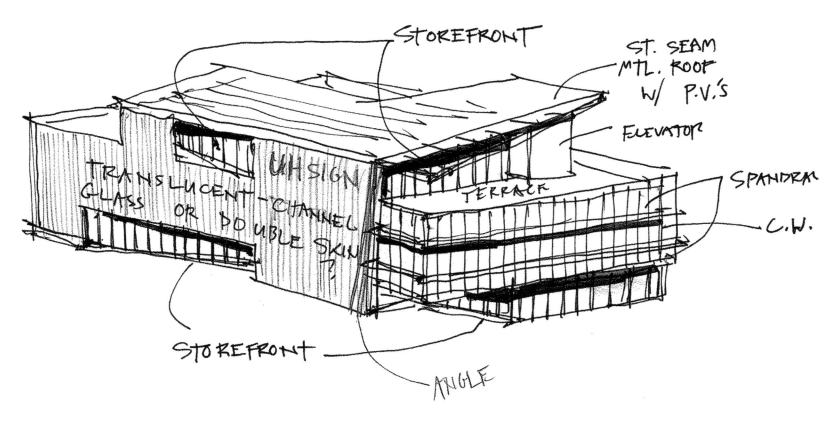

Labels on sketch:

STOREFRONT

ST. SEAM MTL. ROOF W/ P.V.'S

ELEVATOR

SPANDRA

C.W.

TERRACE

UH SIGN

TRANSLUCENT CHANNEL GLASS OR DOUBLE SKIN?

STOREFRONT

ANGLE

Technology Center of Excellence

Client Name: Midmark

Project Size: 100,000 sq. ft.

Cost: $17,000,000

Location: Versailles, Ohio

Role: Design Architect/Architect of Record –
      Moody Nolan

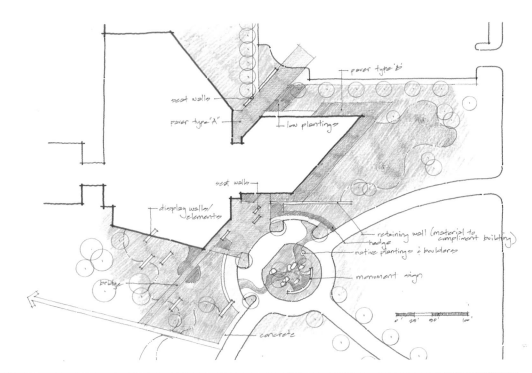

MOODY NOLAN DESIGN

Woodlawn Health and Wellness Center

Client Name: Friend Family Health Center

Project Size: 25,850 sq. ft.

Cost: $8,000,000

Location: Chicago, Illinois

Role: Design Architect/Architect of Record – Moody Nolan

The Residences at Topiary Park Motorists Mixed-Use Development

Client Name: Motorist Insurance Group Realty/
The Robert Weiler Company

Project Size: 92 units

Cost: $20,000,000

Location: Columbus, Ohio

Role: Design Architect/Architect of Record – Moody Nolan

KITCHEN & BAR
GLASS COOK TOP
2 OR 3 PERSON EAT IN BAR
FULL SIZE REFRIGERATOR
DRAWER STYLE MICROWAVE
RETICULATING RANGE-HOOD
SLIDING CABINET DOORS
FULL HEIGHT PANTRY

LIVING ROOM
BUILT-IN TV UNIT
STORAGE

BATHROOM
VANITY & MIRROR
TOILET
FULL SIZE SHOWER & TUB

BONUS LIVING ROOM
BUILT-IN TV UNIT
STORAGE

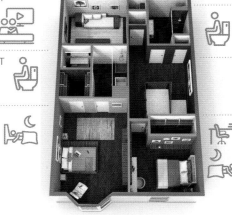

BATHROOM & CLOSET
VANITY & MIRROR
TOILET
FULL SIZE SHOWER & TUB

BEDROOM
BUILT-IN BED PLATFORM
UNDER BED STORAGE
STORAGE
TV OR GIMBEL ARM MOUNT

BATHROOM
VANITY & MIRROR
TOILET
FULL SIZE SHOWER & TUB

BEDROOM & OFFICE
BUILT-IN BED PLATFORM
UNDER BED STORAGE
BUILT-IN DESK UNIT
STORAGE
TV OR GIMBEL ARM MOUNT

SOUTH

FOURTH FLOOR
132'-0"
THIRD FLOOR
121'-4"
SECOND FLOOR
110'-8"
FIRST FLOOR
100'-0"
LOWER LEVEL
90'-0"

WEST

FOURTH FLOOR
132'-0"
THIRD FLOOR
121'-4"
SECOND FLOOR
110'-8"
FIRST FLOOR
100'-0"
LOWER LEVEL
90'-0"

EAST

FOURTH FLOOR
132'-0"
THIRD FLOOR
121'-4"
SECOND FLOOR
110'-8"
FIRST FLOOR
100'-0"
LOWER LEVEL
90'-0"

NORTH

FOURTH FLOOR
132'-0"
THIRD FLOOR
121'-4"
SECOND FLOOR
110'-8"
FIRST FLOOR
100'-0"
LOWER LEVEL
90'-0"

The Black House

Client Name: Northwestern University

Project Size: 8,900 sq. ft.

Cost: $4,500,000

Location: Evanston, Illinois

Role: Design Architect/Architect of Record –
Moody Nolan

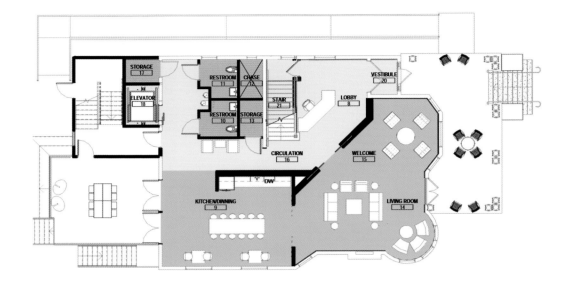

MOODY NOLAN DESIGN

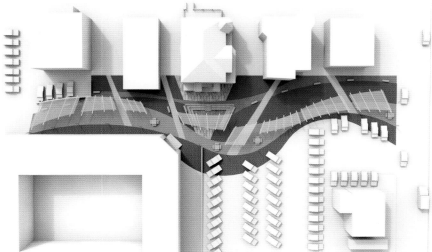

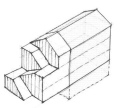

Legacy House

Client Name: Confidential

Project Size: 750 sq. ft.

Cost: Confidential

Location: Columbus, Ohio

Role: Design Architect/Architect of Record –
    Moody Nolan

Linden Empowerment/ Recreation Center

Client Name: City of Columbus Recreation and Parks Department

Project Size: 55,000 sq. ft.

Cost: $15,300,000

Location: Columbus, Ohio

Role: Design Architect/Architect of Record – Moody Nolan

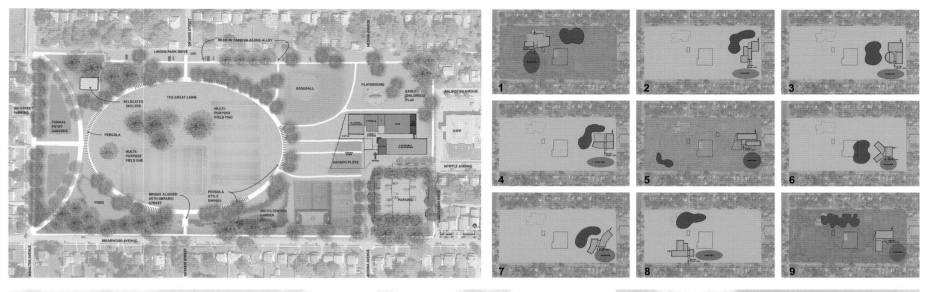

Fifth Third Arena Renovations

Client Name: University of Cincinnati

Project Size: 257,630 sq. ft.

Cost: $85,000,000

Location: Cincinnati, Ohio

Role: Architect of Record – Moody Nolan
    Design Architect – Populous

Football Stadium

Client Name: Temple University

Project Size: 441,000 sq. ft.

Location: Philadelphia, Pennsylvania

Role: Design Architect/Architect of Record Moody Nolan
Sports Planning Architect – AECOM

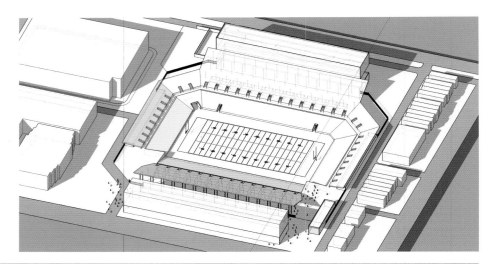

Campus Expansion and Renovation

Client Name: Memorial Health

Project Size: 72,000 sq. ft. Patient Tower, 36,000 sq. ft. Ambulatory Health Center

Cost: $35,500,000

Location: Marysville, Ohio

Role: Design Architect/Architect of Record – Moody Nolan
        Programming & Design Consultant – HOK

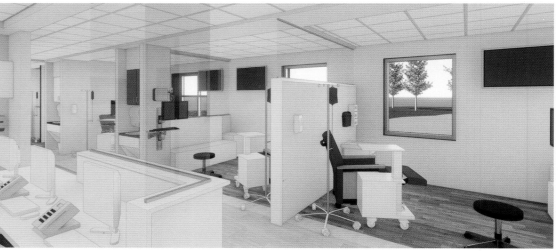

Partners

Front Row:
Paul Pryor, AIA, NCARB, LEED AP, Partner | Director of Construction Administration
Brian Tibbs, AIA, NOMA, NCARB, Partner
Jonathan Moody, AIA, NOMA, NCARB, LEED AP, Partner | President
Curtis J. Moody, FAIA, NOMA, NCARB, LEED AP, Partner | CEO
Bea Thompson, AIA, Partner | Director of Nashville Operations
Renauld D. Mitchell, AIA, NOMA, NCARB, LEED AP BD+C, Partner | Director of Chicago and Washington D.C. Operations
Eileen Goodman, NCIDQ, Partner | Director of Interior Design
Jay Boone, AIA, Partner | Director of General Architecture

Back Row:
Mark J. Bodien, AIA, NCARB, LEED AP, Partner | Director of Sports, Recreation and Student Focused Facilities
Troy Sherrard, FAIA, NCARB, LEED AP, Partner | Practice Leader, Sports and Recreation Design
David King, CPA, Partner | Chief Financial Officer
Todd B. Dove, Principal | Director of Retail Studio
Steven C. Glass, AIA, LEED AP, Principal | Director of Architectural Operations/Risk Management
Allen Schaffer, AIA, NCARB, LEED AP BD+C, WELL AP, LBC Ambassador, Principal | Director of Sustainable Design
Robert K. Larrimer, AIA, NCARB, LEED AP, Partner | Executive Director of Architecture

Appendix

Photography Credits

Current Ideas

You can check out more of our work using the QR codes below.
Just take a picture with your iPhone or use your QR code app
with your Android to view a series of 360-degree images that
will make it feel as if you are walking through one of our projects.
We've been offering this service since 2017 because it provides
clients and prospective clients with a faster, more interactive
experience. Enjoy!

AEROSMITH

THE FALL AND RISE OF

OMNIBUS PRESS
LONDON · NEW YORK · SYDNEY

MARK PUTTERFORD

Copyright © 1991 Omnibus Press
(A Division of Book Sales Limited)

Edited by Chris Charlesworth
Cover and book designed by Four Corners Design:
Lisa Pettibone, Robert Fairclough
Picture research by Paul Giblin

ISBN 0.7119.2303.5
Order No. OP 46028

Exclusive distributors:

Book Sales Limited,
8/9 Frith Street,
London W1V 5TZ, UK.

Music Sales Corporation
225 Park Avenue South
New York, NY 10003, USA

Music Sales Pty Ltd.,
120 Rothschild Avenue,
Rosebery, NSW 2018, Australia.

To the Music Trade only:
Music Sales Limited,
8/9 Frith Street,
London W1V 5TZ, UK.

Photo credits:

All Action: 4, 63b, 76t; Richard Bellia: 5, 7br; Steve Double: front
cover, 1, 62t; Bob Gruen: rear cover, 8, 17,18, 19b, 20b, 23, 24,
26/7, 29b, 34, 39; Imperial Press: 49t; London Features
International: 10r, 11c&b, 12c, 14, 16, 21, 29, 31, 33c, 36, 37, 38,
43, 45, 55, 58, 59b, 61, 63t, 64b, 65t, 66l, 67t&b, 68, 69, 72bl&br,
74, 75t; Michael Ochs Archives: 9t; Pictorial Press: 64t; Barry
Plummer: 32, 33t, 71; Redferns: 20t, 70; Relay: 9c, 12t, 19t, 53,
56c&b, 65b, 72tr, 76b, 78, 80; Retna: 2, 6, 7, 40, 47, 52b, 56t, 60,
62b, 77; Rex Features: 11t, 65c, 73tl; Starfile: 15, 42, 44, 49c&b,
50, 51, 52t, 57, 59t, 66r, 67c, 72tl, 73tr&br, 75c&b.

Typeset by Saxon Printing, Derby
Printed by Ebenezer Baylis & Son Ltd, Worcester

Every effort has been made to trace the copyright holders of the
photographs in this book but one or two were unreachable.
We would be grateful if the photographers concerned would
contact us.

CONTENTS

THIS BOOK WAS WRITTEN IN London during the summer of 1990, despite the World Cup, an iffy Amstrad and the miserable efforts of a childish and small-minded few who went to extraordinary lengths in their attempts to abort the project. Sad, but true.

Nevertheless, while the author's previously untainted opinion of Aerosmith was torn to shreds by the aforementioned few, faith in human kindness and generosity was restored by those who offered invaluable help. A big thank you to all those mentioned below, and a few who aren't. You know who you are ... cheers.

For being decent enough to give me the time of day: Henry Smith, Ray Tabano, Doug Smith, Richard Ogden, Jimmy Crespo, Rick Dufay, Rich Goulberty, Bob Czaykowski, Gary Lyons and Steven Tyler.

For an assortment of favours and other drink-earning deeds: 'Mad' Malcolm Dome, Sylvie Simmons, Darren Winston, Lonn Friend and *RIP* magazine, Betsy Alexander, 'Flipping' Phil Alexander, Richard Cole, Pete Makowski, Ross Halfin, Scott Koenig, Arlett Vereecke, Xavier Russell, Lemmy, Nikki Sixx and all those who provided me with quotes. Sod those who didn't.

For the music: Steven Tyler, Joe Perry, Brad Whitford, Tom Hamilton, Joey Kramer, Jimmy Crespo and Rick Dufay.

For his patience and editorial judgement: Chris Charlesworth.

For sustenance: Jack Daniel's Old No. 7.

For everything else: Lynn Seager.

For nothing: NO THANKS to Tim Collins Management, who not only refused the author access to the band but contrived to block every avenue of research they could and even tried to prevent the publishers from obtaining photographs of the band.

This book is dedicated to Joan Putterford.

Lest we forget those who didn't make it: Johnny Ace, Duane Allman, Mel Appleby, Florence Ballard, Carlton Barrett, Stiv Bator, Duster Bennett, Bill Black, Mike Bloomfield, Marc Bolan, Tommy Bolin, Graham Bond, John Bonham, David Blue, Tim Buckley, Paul Butterfield, Cliff Burton, David Byron, Robert Calvert, Karen Carpenter, Mama Cass, John Cippolina, Harry Chapin, Steve Clark, Jim Croce, Eddie Cochran, Allan Collins, Sam Cooke, Vincent Crane, Ian Curtis, King Curtis, Tom Evans, Pete De Freitas, Sandy Denny, Nick Drake, Pete Farndon, Tom Fogerty, Allan Freed, Bobby Fuller, Steve Gaines, Cassie Gaines, Marvin Gaye, Lowell George, Andy Gibb, John Glascock, Rik Grech, Bill Haley, Pete Ham, Tim Hardin, Alex Harvey, Les Harvey, Donny Hathaway, Jimi Hendrix, Bob Hite, Buddy Holly, Gary Holton, James Honeyman-Scott, Al Jackson, James Jamerson, Eric 'Stumpy Joe', Robert Johnson, Brian Jones, Janis Joplin, Terry Kath, Johnny Kidd, Alexis Korner, Paul Kossoff, Martin Lamble, John Lennon, Frankie Lymon, Phil Lynott, Bob Marley, Richard Manuel, Robbie McIntosh, Jimmy McCulloch, Brent Mydland, Keith Moon, Jim Morrison, Nico, Rick Nelson, Berry Oakley, Phil Ochs, Roy Orbison, Malcolm Owen, Felix Pappalardi, Gram Parsons, Jaco Pastorius, 'Stumpy' Pepys, Pigpen, Elvis Presley, Carl Radle, Razzle, Otis Redding, Terry Reid, Keith Relf, Randy Rhoads, J. P. Richardson, Minnie Riperton, John Rostill, Bon Scott, Hillal Slovak, Del Shannon, Ian Stewart, Rory Storm, Stu Sutcliffe, Tammi Terrell, Gary Thain, Peter Tosh, Richie Valens, Ronnie Van Zant, Stevie Ray Vaughan, Sid Vicious, Gene Vincent, Muddy Waters, Paul Williams, Al Wilson, Dennis Wilson, Jackie Wilson, Ricky Wilson, Clarence White, Danny Whitten, Andrew Wood, Chris Wood and more.

Mark Putterford, November 1990.

SWEET EMOTION

T'S SATURDAY AUGUST 18, 1990, D-Day – or Donington Day – to anyone with hair past their shoulder, and inside the fences of the famous Donington Park motor-racing circuit in the east Midlands of England, 80,000 people are bearing witness to a remarkable phenomenon, nay, a miracle.

It's not raining.

More than that, the sun is shining on a band for whom life has been a ferocious storm of success and failure, adulation and addiction, achievement and abuse, supreme distinction and rampant self-destruction.

A band who shamelessly adopted the legacy of their British peers, wrapped it up in American rags and razzmatazz, and sold it to a global generation of rockers, rollers and backstreet strollers.

A band who not only went to the edge and looked down, but who pelted headlong over the precipice with all guitars blazing and all systems overloading, only to smash into a million shattered fragments of disarray, disaster and despair.

Aerosmith. The living, screaming, kicking proof of rock 'n' roll resurrection. Ghosts of a rampant renaissance, dancing on the grave of their drug-blurred past. A musical miracle, no less.

Today, everyone is straining for a glimpse of Aerosmith. From the stage, a tiny shell-like plateau dwarfed by twin tower blocks of PA, the

sea of faces looks like a claustrophobic nightmare, stretching awesomely into the distance. Union Jacks twirl slowly, homemade banners wave at the huge yellow-on-black Aerosmith logo backdrop billowing in the early evening breeze, and the stomping sounds of top-notch rock whips small pockets of anxious spectators into sporadic chants and cheers.

A hundred yards away, in the backstage enclosure of yellow Portacabin dressing rooms, the Aerosmith entourage – a small cluster of wives, children, management officials, VIP guests and security gorillas – begins to move as one. A film crew follows, cameras flash like firecrackers, but the band stroll hand-in-hand with their wives with well-versed nonchalance. These are veteran rock soldiers marching unto war, much less tin troops to the slaughter.

Eventually the gaggle of guests reaches the huge scaffolding construction that is the stage and slowly climbs the steep steel steps. A good luck kiss here, a wave there, and the gang splits, band stage left, others stage right. Something stirs . . .

An avalanche of cheers. Thundering anticipation. An eruption of relief. Blinding ecstasy. Aerosmith on stage. Sweet emotion . . .

Steven Tyler, the face that raunched a thousand hips, is the magnetic focal point of it all. Impossibly fit at 42, he's the perennial rock 'n' roll ragamuffin; dressed like a Las Vegas hooker on acid in dandy designer white rags, with a tear painted beneath his left eye, he looks like a stray squirt of toothpaste as he wriggles around his domain with scarf-adorned microphone-stand trailing behind every exaggerated move. From behind you can see his back muscles tensing with every note he screams, as his ridiculously large lips droop and curl around the mike like he's french-kissing a fat-lipped whore. And then there's the voice, a tonsil-wringing rasp that'd peel the paint off a new car at a hundred paces.

Once slammed for being little more than a Mick Jagger impersonator – the lips, the leotards, the strut, the both-singing-into-the-same-microphone stunt with his Keith Richards-like foil, Joe Perry – Steven Tyler has long since established himself as one of rock's finest frontmen, with perhaps only David Lee Roth standing in the way of his elevation to a class of his own. If Jagger was ever this entertaining, this energetic, this outrageously cool, no one in the Donington audience would remember it.

On his left stands Joe Perry, disgustingly healthy with taut, flyweight-like muscles and a beach-bum tan to prove it, ripping notes off his

Below, left: Steven Tyler with wife Teresa and daughter Chelsea Anna, backstage at Donington.

fretboard with arrogant aplomb. With his jutting, mafia-mobster jaw-line, unruly mop of shiny black hair and studied, stone-faced stare, he looks every inch the rock star, cooler than a fortnight in Finland. And he knows it.

Meanwhile, Perry's guitar sidekick Brad Whitford goes about his business with an alarming lack of fuss, laying down the lightning rhythms with a doleful expression that never changes the expression on his oversized and now smartly bearded face.

And then there's the impregnable backbone of Tom Hamilton and Joey Kramer; the former tall, willowy and cucumber-cool, blond hair blowing in the breeze while his long fingers crawl across his bass like an albino tarantula; the latter short, stocky and powerfully percussive, an impish grin on his face as he gazes from atop his drum-kit out across the adoring masses.

With the help of part-time member Thom Gimble on keyboards and saxophone, the band trot out all the highpoints of their latest multi-million-selling platter, 'Pump', and the audience – swollen into millions by a live national broadcast on the BBC's Radio One – greets each song like an old friend.

In the hospitality tents backstage, guests, music industry bods and assorted middle-aged mutant hero liggers huddle around the close-circuit TV sets to keep up with the action out-front. On the side of the stage a privileged few with gold-dust passes stare bug-eyed and knock-kneed at the exciting scenes. Family members dance and clap along (although Tyler's baby daughter Chelsea Anna, complete with miniature 'Pump' tour jacket and ear-muffs, looks on rather bemused). The members of Poison, who preceded Aerosmith on the Donington bill – which also featured Whitesnake, Quireboys and Thunder – mouth the words to every song and turn to grin at each other every time Tyler completes one of his microphone-twirling tricks. And an old-looking but smartly-dressed and somewhat familiar gent stands leaning against a scaffolding pole, pushing his head back and forth violently in time to the beat, with lips pursed and eyes squinting . . .

The man is Jimmy Page, the former Yardbird and Led Zeppelin guitarist whose influence on Aerosmith can be traced way back to the sixties, when one of Tyler's first bands supported The Yardbirds on their visits to the East Coast of America. Now, in an ironic twist of fate, the wheel has turned full circle and Aerosmith play host to Page on his home turf, inviting him on-stage for a jam on the old Yardbirds classic 'Train Kept A Rollin''. When he steps out and launches into the first few notes, Tyler turns to Joey Kramer and mouths the words ''I can't believe it!'' and the magic moment is etched all over his face.

Finally, Tyler sits with a keyboard on a riser high above the Kramer kit for a poignant version of 'Dream On', the power-ballad that gave Aerosmith their first hit single in America, and then it's a swagger through 'Walk This Way', their first British hit, before Tyler concludes proceedings with his usual back-flipping, age-defying gymnastics, and the band take a bow and leave to ecstatic applause.

As they saunter down the ramp at the back of the stage, Tyler already fussing over his baby, Concorde roars by startlingly low overhead on its way from Heathrow airport to New York, and the Aerosmith entourage stand and stare with dumbfounded amazement at its incredible timing.

''Hey, beat that for a finale!'' Tyler shouts at the author above the incredible din, and he breaks into a wide Cheshire cat grin that even has little Chelsea Anna gurgling happily.

Yet not even a respectful fly-past by Concorde could've upstaged this particular Aer-show, forged as it was from the benefits of fighting-fit sobriety and new-found professionalism. Had this been the seventies the band would probably have been clouded in an alcoholic and drug-induced haze, more interested in the tarty talent backstage than exploiting their own on-stage. But this, of all the supergroup reunions which speckled the eighties, is without doubt the greatest comeback story in the history of rock 'n' roll: a band hitting its creative and commercial peak during its 20th anniversary year, long after it had been written off and left for dead by even its most loyal followers.

It must be, as Steven Tyler laughingly suggested during the Donington mêlée, ''The Lord's way of showing that even He's an Aerosmith fan!''

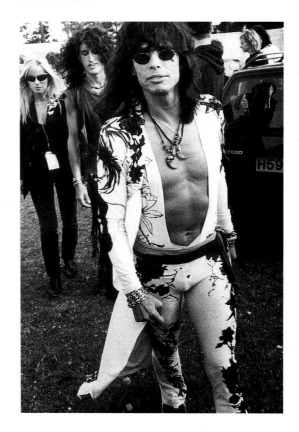

CHAPTER TWO

TALES FROM THE ATTIC

SOMEHOW, STEVEN TYLER always knew he was destined for immortality. It was a childhood obsession that first took tangible form when he chiselled his initials into a huge boulder near his parents' holiday home of Trow-Rico, in Sunapee, New Hampshire. It represented, those with a penchant for appalling puns might argue, his first vision of being eternal in rock . . .

Born Steven Victor Tallarico in Polyclinic Hospital, New York City, on March 26, 1948 – just three years after the end of World War Two – the young Italian-American had music in his genes. His grandfather, Giovani Tallarico, played chamber music in the ballrooms of grand hotels in the twenties, and under his tuition, his father Victor became a classical pianist and teacher who went to Juilliard and even played at New York's famous Carnegie Hall. Steven grew up under the grand piano listening to his father playing scales and dreaming of taking the family tradition to even greater heights.

At school, Roosevelt High in the Yonkers district of New York, the Tallarico boy found it difficult to crystallise his aspirations. "I was a freak, an ultimate nerd," he later admitted, and stories of his getting kicked out of his Physical Science class for chasing a little girl with a broken light bulb would seem to justify this description. Steven himself also became the target of physical attacks in school, taunted by classmates who christened him 'nigger lips'.

Steven felt most at home at his parents' 360-acre resort house near Boston, in New Hampshire. He'd spend his summer vacations there, stocking the pond with trout, playing in the hayloft and mowing the lawns in what sounds like a chapter from one of Tom Sawyer's adventures.

"I was an overactive, hyper nerd," he recalls. "I got into everything, I bothered everybody, I did everything to the max. If I saw a bug, I squished it and ate it. If I saw a dead animal on the side of the road, I went over and pulled its teeth out and wore them around my neck. I wanted to get into everything."

He even started to get into 'illegal substances' during his mid-teens and shouldered the shame of

being busted for drug possession at school. He was eventually moved to Quintano's, a place for 'the creative child who couldn't get along with the regular system'. Like he said, he was a freak.

But most significantly of all he wanted to get into music, and it wasn't long before he was entertaining the folk at Trow-Rico with his pantomime based on 'Animal Crackers' and singing 'There's a hole in my bucket, Eliza' at the Saturday night skits his aunt Phyllis put on in the recreation hall.

Nevertheless, the adolescent Tallarico's first 'proper' gig was with his father's Lester Lanin-style swing band in a grand hotel called the Sunapee Lodge. Steven had taught himself to play the drums to what he terms 'society music'. While he kept the beat Steven's earliest audience danced the lindy and the foxtrot.

Back in Yonkers during school terms where he hung out with the Green Mountain Boys gang, the kid with the big lips and an overwhelming urge to show off began to think about forming his own band. He'd been turned on to this thing called rock 'n' roll by the new bands, most notably The Beatles and The Rolling Stones, that were suddenly springing up in England. First there was a group called The Maniacs, then YAKS . . . and then The Strangeurs, formed around the beginning of 1964 and Steven's first serious group.

The Strangeurs, aptly named even today as it included such unknowns as Peter Stahl on guitar, Alan Stromeyer on bass and Don Soloman on keyboards, featured the 16-year-old Tallarico doubling up on drums and lead vocals (after he heard Stromeyer singing The Beach Boys' 'In My Room' and thought he could do better). They were typical of the young bands bred by the American bar circuit, destined to play covers that ranged from patchy versions of songs like Van Morrison's 'Gloria' to 'Wild Thing' by The Troggs and other material from the repertoires of The Animals, The Byrds, The Pretty Things, The Stones and more. Tallarico led from the back, a microphone stand bent uncomfortably over his shoulder to enable him to be heard above the rough edged backing.

"In my mind I was always a rock star," he told *Q* magazine in 1989. "I would pretend I knew what it was like to be in an established band. I still have clippings at home of The Strangeurs. 'Steven Tyler, his lower lip hanging like Jagger's, brought the front row to its feet.' I was 16, but I was playing rock star even when the music sounded like bad Freddie And The Dreamers."

By this time, however, The Strangeurs had run into some complications with their name. It transpired that there was another similarly named band working in the Manhattan area, and so, after briefly re-naming themselves Thee Strangeurs, they finally settled on the new and hipper sounding title of Chain Reaction to avoid the confusion.

Before long Tallarico developed a promising writing partnership with Don Soloman, and a swelling stockpile of original material helped complement the band's regular covers, putting a

professional sheen on Chain Reaction's burgeoning style. They eventually began to get gigs with many of the 'happening' bands that passed through New York: The Byrds, The Beach Boys (a gig Steven did with his flies undone throughout!), and the third incarnation of The Yardbirds with young Jimmy Page leading the band on guitar, a stint that later had Tallarico claiming, somewhat tongue-in-cheek, he'd been Led Zeppelin's first roadie . . .

"It was in the last vestiges of The Yardbirds, just before Page left to form Zeppelin, and the band were playing at the Anderson Theatre in New York City, just across the street from the Fillmore. Back in those days, if you were well known in a particular town and a band like The Yardbirds came to your town, you got to open up for them. Anyway, The Yardbirds came to play a gig at Staples High School in Connecticut, and we (Chain Reaction) used to play at Staples, so we got the chance to open for them. We ended up doing that for four shows, through Connecticut, Boston and New York.

"What happened was, when you travelled from show to show like that you put all the amps and things in a small truck or station wagon – it wasn't 'big time' like it is now with huge trucks – and we shared a wagon between us. Of course, back then all the musicians had to hump their own gear . . . but looking back at it with today's eyes, when you hump gear you're a roadie, right? So I guess you can say that I was a roadie for The Yardbirds . . . and if you want you can say that they were roadies for me, too!"

As they learnt from them and others in live situations, Chain Reaction cut a single in their efforts to emulate their British heroes. They recorded 'The Sun' for the Date Forecast label with producer Arty Traum (who, along with brother Happy Traum was an important figure in the New York folk scene of the early sixties), and they also put down a song called 'You Should've Been Here

Far left: Aerosmith circa 1973; left to right: Joe Perry, Steven Tyler, Joey Cramer, Brad Whitford and Tom Hamilton.
Top: Steven Tyler (extreme left) with Chain Reaction during the mid 1960s.
Bottom: Tyler in 1990.

Yesterday' (b/w 'Ever Loving Man') under the production guidance of Gene Radice, whose son Mark, then four-years-old, would later slip into the Aerosmith picture by playing keyboards during the band's 1978 American tour.

These early attempts at busting the *Billboard* charts, it has to be said, weren't entirely successful – although, rumour has it, 'The Sun' did reasonably well in Italy! Tallarico and Soloman eventually left Chain Reaction to form another band, William Proud, and continued to play the local small hall-type venues to no avail. But nevertheless, to those who encountered Tallarico and his freakish friends in the late sixties, decked out as they were in their dandy Carnaby Street rags with hippy-long hair, they were the nearest thing Sunapee had to rock stars.

In particular, one young lad who worked in a local ice-cream parlour called The Anchorage saw them as the epitome of rock stardom – loud, obnoxious hooligans who seemed determined to be the centre of attention wherever they went. When they visited his ice cream parlour they'd throw food around like deranged chimps at a tea-party, and he'd have to clear up after them – something he's never forgotten. His name was Joe Perry.

* * *

Anthony Joseph Perry was born on September 10, 1950, in Lawrence, Massachusetts, and like Tallarico was induced into music by his family. His uncle had built his own acoustic guitar and Joe would mess about on it, playing along to Beatles and Roy Orbison songs. And while his parents tried to tempt him into a more classical line of musical training, giving him piano and clarinet lessons, it was the guitar that he was most interested in – the Chuck Berry brand of guitar

playing that is, and not the flamenco style that his parents favoured.

Like many kids, Perry saw rock 'n' roll as an escape – '''River Deep Mountain High' (by Ike And Tina Turner) was the theme tune of my adolescence,'' he once said – and after testing the water with The Beatles he delved deeper to discover bands like The Ventures and The Yardbirds, and then later Ten Years After and Deep Purple, a progression towards heavier tastes which reflected the tastes of the kids he hung out with in his teens.

At high school he played in a band called Flash who played primitive gigs at parties. ''We used to go around and play in this kid's garage,'' he told *RIP* magazine last year, ''and we'd rehearse with the door of the garage open, so people could come by and hear us. This kid had an older brother in college, and he said 'Well, we gotta play at this frat house, and not only are they gonna give us free beer, but they're gonna give us $5 each!' I said 'Why?' He said, 'Well, you get paid, you know!' And I said 'What a great thing!' It never occurred to me that you could actually make money or see something from it other than the pleasure of playing. But it was great to be able to get a little money to pay for guitar strings and gas for the car.''

Perry's parents, however, were concerned about the way their son was growing up. He wasn't a particularly good scholar, and even a move to a prep school didn't seem to have any effect on him. Never managing to graduate, Perry eventually found work in a local foundry for just over two dollars an hour, a job he managed to

hold down for two years, despite 'horror show' memories of that whole period.

Finally, Perry decided to jack the job in and move to New Hampshire where, like Tallarico, his parents owned a holiday home. To pay for his keep and support his hobby of music, he took part-time jobs, one of which was washing dishes at The Anchorage to rake in a few cents. It was there that he met a tall blond lad who lived in the area and shared the same taste in music, not to mention ice cream, and who had a pretty decent grasp of the bass guitar. Between them they decided to put a band together, interestingly christened Pipe Dream, and thus, unwittingly, another chunk of rock history began to take shape.

* * *

Perry's new pal was Thomas William Hamilton, born on December 31, 1951 in Colorado Springs, Colorado, the son of an Air Force worker. Because his father would periodically be stationed in different towns, Hamilton and his family travelled around the country a lot, but long before he moved to New Hampshire he'd been bitten by the rock 'n' roll bug.

In fact, Hamilton claims he was just four-years-old when he remembers seeing his older brother, head down, legs spread-eagled, playing 'Peter Gunn' on his first guitar. He thought it was "the coolest thing I ever saw" and persuaded his brother to teach him a few chords. Later he'd sneak into his brother's room and borrow his Fender Stratocaster and amplifier, his fascination for the sounds he could get out of this new box of tricks knowing no bounds.

Even by the time he was eight Hamilton had become fascinated by a band who emulated The Ventures, America's top instrumental pop/rock group in the pre-Beatles era which had also inspired Joe Perry early on. But for the budding bassist it was seeing The Beatles on the *Ed Sullivan Show* in America during the early sixties that really convinced him his future was in music. He immediately rushed out and bought 'Meet The Beatles' and spent the next few years checking out all of The Beatles' contemporaries, particularly The Rolling Stones, before eventually graduating to the harder blues-rock bands which blossomed around the Woodstock age.

"I was a fanatical music fan," he later confessed. "I'm from a really small town in the country, and one of my only ways to really get off was to get my favourite new Beatles or Stones album and play it about 20 times. Then I went to see Cream at the Psychedelic Supermarket and was completely blown away by them. After that

every weekend I'd go to concerts in Boston, and even the equipment trucks outside concerts would give me a big rush. I don't think I ever saw a band in that period of time that I thought was bad because I'd get off on the whole electricity of the situation."

Hamilton's own experience in bands began when he was 13, when he joined a high school fun outfit called The Mosquitoes, named not surprisingly with the sensational Beatles in mind. But then, with the onset of psychedelia throwing up groups with increasingly ridiculous monickers, he found himself in one called The Merciless Tangerine, a blues-based act which went through a number of permutations on its one-way journey into obscurity.

After meeting Joe Perry his fortunes took a turn for the better. He was 14 when Pipe Dream began playing their first, ramshackle gigs, but over the next couple of years they would make steady progress, first through an outfit called Plastic Glass, and then to The Jam Band, a raunchier, rough-around-the-edges set-up who played covers of songs by The MC5, Yardbirds, Jimi Hendrix, Cream and Ten Years After, and who would soon capture the imagination of Steven Tallarico.

"We weren't into melodies too much," Perry recalls. "We just banged out the tunes and made it up as we went along. I always liked to create mayhem and have unlimited energy, smash up guitars, go crazy and play as loud and as fast as I could. That was the thing Steven liked about me when he first saw me, because he was mainly into perfecting arrangements and getting it just right. I guess that was the combination which made Aerosmith *Aerosmith*."

Perry first invited Tallarico down to check out The Jam Band at a local Sunapee club called The Barn in the summer of 1970. The band were excited because to them Tallarico, with his ultra professional approach and strikingly fashionable looks, was the real thing. "He'd even put out a record for God's sake," Hamilton remembers, "and that was the ultimate to us." But Tallarico was somewhat less impressed with what he saw . . . until the band did their version of Fleetwood Mac's 'Rattlesnake Shake'.

"I said to myself, 'That's it. These guys suck – they can't even tune a guitar – but they have a great groove going.' I knew if I could show them a little of what I knew, with the looseness they had, then we'd really have something."

Tallarico made up his mind to join forces with Perry and Hamilton shortly afterwards, initially

luck there.''

Tabano owned a leather store in Boston where he and his girlfriend made and sold leather outfits for the trendier city slickers. The band, meanwhile, set about the arduous task of auditioning drummers, but by a stroke of extraordinary luck the man they were looking for just happened to walk into Ray's leather store one day . . .

''I'd known Joey Kramer since high school,'' says Ray, ''because the brother of the guitar player in The Dantes used to play with Joey in a band called The King Bees. So Joey comes in and goes, 'Hey, I hear you're looking for a drummer', so I took him down to an audition one day . . . and that's how Aerosmith began.''

* * *

Joseph Michael Kramer, born on June 21, 1950, in The Bronx, New York, had wanted to be a drummer since his eighth grade. He actually got to know Tallarico in 1965, when his father wouldn't let him have a drum kit and he asked Steven, then drumming with The Strangeurs, if he could borrow his. But he soon acquired one of his own, albeit against his parents' wishes, and knew exactly where he wanted to head. From ninth to twelfth grade he went to six or seven different schools, but by now his studying had taken a back seat to his music, and later he'd be forced to confess: ''I made it through high school by the skin of my teeth!''

Kramer's early stage experience with bands like The Turnpikes, Unique 4 and The King Bees also involved playing covers of Cream and Jimi Hendrix songs, the kind of typically self-indulgent late sixties blues-rock which called for ludicrously long solos. But he also got into soul music through Detroit's Tamla Motown label and played with black bands while in Boston, most notably the embryonic Tavares (destined to have limited chart success in the seventies: remember 'Heaven Must Be Missing An Angel'?) which, he has always maintained, ''taught me a lot about groove, accent and choreography.''

But rock 'n' roll was always Joey Kramer's first love, and the chance to join forces with Tallarico and his friends came at just the right time for him. He'd been studying at the Berkeley School Of Music in Boston and had carefully refined his technique, but he was desperate to hit the road with a 'real' rock band. When he was offered the job with this new outfit, as yet unnamed, he was unconvinced by the racket made by Joe Perry and Tom Hamilton and unsure whether or not to throw in his lot with them. But, as Hamilton himself recalls, ''As soon as he found out Steven was going to be in the band he took a different attitude.''

By the end of 1970 the five were ensconced in a

intending to replace the departing Pudge Scott on drums and vocals. But, aware of the visual restrictions of a drummer/vocalist and keen to develop the showman side of his extrovert nature, Tallarico suggested the band looked for another drummer, as well as a rhythm guitarist. The band would later audition for a suitable stickman, but for the rhythm guitarist's role Tallarico put forward the name of his colleague in William Proud, Ray Tabano.

Raymond Tabano was born on December 23, 1946, in The Bronx, New York, but moved to Westchester County when he was 12-years-old after his mother remarried. A year later he started hanging out with the then 11-year-old Steven Tallarico, who lived just around the block in the same neighbourhood, and the two became fast friends at Roosevelt High, sharing the same interests in gymnastics and, of course, music.

''I remember when we started rival bands at school,'' Ray recalls, ''his (Chain Reaction) was a Beatles-type band, very slick and conservatively dressed. I was the bass player in a Stones-type band, with long hair, wild clothes an' everything, called The Dantes. Later Steven left Roosevelt to go to a professional high school, but when Chain Reaction began to fall apart I kind of drifted back into the picture with Steven and I started working with his bands. When I was 19 I moved to Massachusetts, and we got a band called William Proud together. We'd go up to New Hampshire to play, and we'd also play around the islands in New York, that sort of thing. But when Steven mentioned he'd met these guys called Joe Perry and Tom Hamilton who he wanted to form a band with, I suggested we moved to Boston, to try our

"They're fantastic — one of the few bands I'd go out of my way to see."

BRUCE DICKINSON, IRON MAIDEN

Left: Joey Kramer (below) during the 1970s and (above) in the 1980s. Above: Original Aerosmith guitarist Ray Tabano at home in Yonkers in 1990. Below right: Tabano during his time with Aerosmith.

dingy, damp and decidedly dodgy three-bedroomed apartment at 1325 Commonwealth Avenue in Boston; excited, anxious young men trying to keep their heads amid the squalor with a deep-rooted desperation for recognition. Some of them kept their day jobs – Tallarico worked in a bakery, Perry was the part-time caretaker of a synagogue – but times were hard, and the situation conjures up a vision of a sort of American version of *The Young Ones*. Hamilton's bedroom doubled as the living room, Tallarico and Perry shared a tiny room with bunk beds, and they'd live off jelly sandwiches, cheap brown rice and vegetable dishes, with the odd bowl of Campbells soup if they were lucky. When they weren't rehearsing they'd get stoned and listen to Jeff Beck or Deep Purple albums, or watch *The Three Stooges* on TV.

At this time several names were under consideration for the hopeful young outfit – The Hookers was one, probably because Tallarico looked, dressed and shook his butt like one, and Spike Jones, the name of a comic musician, was another which several of the band favoured. But the issue was settled when Joey Kramer suggested a name he'd scrawled across his maths and biology text books in high school. It had nothing to do with Sinclair Lewis' classic novel *Arrowsmith* . . . in fact, Joey didn't know where it came from, but it just sounded good to him and the others. What better reason than that to call the band Aerosmith?

In retrospect it seems to conjure up contrasting images – the lightness of flight with the weight of an anvil – in much the same way that the name Led Zeppelin conjures up a similar picture.

It was during these very early days in Boston that Aerosmith decided that they didn't want to be just another club-circuit band, slogging around in ever decreasing circles doing the usual Top 40

covers so club managers could sell more beer to thirsty, dancing customers. The Boston scene had always been rather sterile as far as rock 'n' roll was concerned, perhaps because of that beer-selling mentality in the clubs, and the painful fact for the city's youngsters to swallow was that even from the early sixties to around 1968, when most big American cities were hotbeds of new rock talent, Boston's profile remained not so much low as subterranean.

Sure, Boston could boast bands like The Remains, The Lost, The Barbarians, The Hallucinations and Teddy And The Pandas, but it did so under its breath rather than at the top of its voice. And when MGM Records coined the phase 'The Bosstown Sound' for groups like Ultimate Spinach, The Beacon Street Union and Orpheus in 1968, it was kidding itself that there was more of a scene than there actually was. In fact, folk music in the James Taylor 'sensitive singer-songwriter' mould was, for an unhealthy period of time, the main source of musical 'hipness' for the no-doubt thick-sweatered and wispy-bearded academic Bostonions.

Blues music, however, did manage to find a finger-hold in Boston society around the turn of the decade. With a few blues clubs beginning to recognise homegrown talent, the J. Geils Bands began to enjoy some acceptance, enough in fact to create a bandwagon on which the rather less memorable likes of The Orphans, The Sidewinders, Reddy Teddy, The James Montgomery Band and The Modern Lovers trundled to no avail.

But the J. Geils Band were making some headway around 1970 (they eventually claimed an international hit in 1982 with 'Centerfold'), and they soon decided to break out of Boston's restrictive conservatism and make a bid for nationwide fame and fortune. This left Boston's

club owners with a gap to fill, but Aerosmith didn't exactly fit the bill, reluctant as they were to knock out all the old standards night after night. They did need the money however, and the clubs paid reasonably well. But Aerosmith were more ambitious than that, and they opted to branch out and play high schools, frat parties and university-type gigs in the suburbs whenever they could, pushing their own songs all the time.

Aerosmith's first gig was at Nipmuc Regional High School in the autumn of 1970. Legend has it Tallarico and Perry argued that very night about Perry playing too loud, thereby ushering in an Aerosmith tradition, but whatever the truth in that, the band's influences were certainly on their sleeves that day, with songs like The Stones' 'Live With Me', The Yardbirds' 'Shapes Of Things' and John Lennon's 'Cold Turkey' finding their way into the set.

Yet for Aerosmith, the most important aspect of their stage set was testing out their own compositions on whoever might find themselves confronted by this rowdy bunch of long-haired hoodlums.

''We used to played at Navy Officers' clubs for all these 'straights','' laughs Hamilton, ''and we'd just go in, play our stuff (like 'Walkin' The Dog' and 'One Way Street' from the band's first album) and rock out. And although these people had never heard the songs before they knew damn well they could dance to them.''

''We'd go and play ski lodges up in New Hampshire, town halls and anywhere people would take us,'' says Ray Tabano. ''We did a gig at Tom's sister's school, we did one in a hall near where Joe's family and friends lived . . . it was hard work, but a lot of fun, because we especially loved seeing how people would react to our own songs.''

The band were also desperately keen to get noticed and would pull stunts like turning up outside Boston University and playing on the spot, aiming for as much press publicity or word-of-mouth notoriety as possible. One person who got to hear of this enterprising and somewhat outrageous local band was Steve Paul who managed The Winter Brothers, Johnny and Edgar, and whose New York nightclub Steve Paul's Scene was at one time a gathering place for New York's rock *cognoscenti*. Looking for a band to open for Edgar Winter and Humble Pie at New York's Academy Of Music, Paul checked Aerosmith out and duly booked them. Their performance, albeit dogged by an awful and bass-less sound, received mixed reviews in the local press but was sufficient to stir up even more interest in the provinces.

Mach Bell, a local Boston singer who was later to join The Joe Perry Project, also remembers

seeing Aerosmith around this time. ''They had a regular Monday night gig at a teen centre, the Lakeview Ballroom in Mendon,'' he says, ''and they'd draw over a thousand or more kids a night, at $2 a head.'' He later approached Tallarico about playing his local town hall and was made aware of the band's requirements: $300 and a box of malted milk balls in their dressing room!

Even though they were earning $300 a night, Aerosmith were still very much struggling under mounting financial pressure, especially since they'd given up their day jobs by now. They were even running out of places to rehearse. Despite the encouragement of an increasingly loyal local following, the reality of life on the bottom rung of rock 'n' roll's cloud-piercing ladder to success was biting into their resolve.

''They worked incredibly hard because they wanted to be rock stars so bad,'' reflects Henry Smith, a friend of the band since the very beginning and a former roadie for The Yardbirds who ended up tour managing Aerosmith during their prime. ''But sometimes they'd question the whole thing, wondering if what they were doing was right. It was really just the sheer hunger they had that kept them going.''

And, it must be said, an almost arrogant self-confidence which had instilled in them the belief that they could square up to almost anyone.

''When we started I imagined that these people like Rick Derringer were like Lord High Doodledums who sat in the corner with servants picking their toes,'' Tyler reflected recently. ''But we played with some of those guys and I knew we had more than they had.''

By 1971, however, Ray Tabano's position in the band was beginning to look shaky. Henry Smith recalls his becoming ''a little too pushy'', and he ended up leaving the band, selling his leather store and moving to Mexico for six months. He would eventually return to the Aerosmith fold two years later after an offer from his old friend Steven, starting off as a roadie but soon becoming Marketing Director, helping to design the now famous 'winged' logo, establishing and presiding over the band's merchandise business and working for several other of Aerosmith's management's acts, including Ted Nugent. But immediately on returning from Mexico, Tabano joined another local Boston band called Justin Tyme who, coincidentally, would soon be opening up for Aerosmith. Yet even more ironic was the fact that the man Tabano replaced in Justin Tyme was the very same guitarist who'd replaced him in Aerosmith! Enter Brad Whitford . . .

* * *

Brad Ernest Whitford, the youngest member of Aerosmith, was born on February 23, 1952 in Winchester, Massachusetts. A quiet, shy youngster, he began playing music on the trumpet at school, but like so many others his world turned upside down the day The Beatles made their infamous appearance on the *Ed Sullivan Show*. His response was to disappear into the basement of his parents' home and make his own guitar, desperate to emulate his new-found idols.

''I've known them since '73 when we shared the same management, and I like them a lot. I think they're a great band.''
LEMMY

Above: Brad Whitford during the 1970s.
Right: Whitford in the 1980s.

When Brad finally bought himself a 'real' guitar he'd begun to learn the chords to standards like Van Morrison's 'Gloria' and The Kingsmen's 'Louie Louie', and then moved on to playing material by The Young Rascals, the New York band led by Felix Cavaliere who became popular in the States after hits with 'Good Lovin'' and 'Groovin'', and Three Dog Night, a poppy US outfit who hit the big time in America during the late sixties with covers of material by Randy Newman, Elton John, Harry Nilsson and Laura Nyro, and early Jimi Hendrix material.

Whitford even wound up at the Berkeley School Of Music in Boston, studying music theory and composition. But he quit after just a year, claiming: ''I thought I'd learn a lot more out in front of people, playing every night.''

Brad had indeed been playing in bands since the age of 16, getting himself into curiously named outfits like Earth Incorporated, The Teapot Dome, The Cymbals Of Resistance and Justin Tyme who, thanks to the endeavours of a good booking agent in Boston, got a lot of work playing local fraternities and canteens, allowing Brad to make enough money to pay back his parents for the loans they took out to buy him his equipment in the first place.

When the job with Aerosmith came up he grabbed it with both hands, providing a fearsome foil for Joe Perry's searing lead licks and adding considerable weight to the raunchy R&B attack of early Aerosmith. It was a smart piece of head hunting by the band, and it signalled an upturn in their fortunes accentuated by the arrival on the scene shortly afterwards of successful Boston promoter Frank Connolly. The band had been rehearsing in Boston's old Fenway Theatre out of the kindness of manager John O'Toole's heart, and O'Toole became so impressed by what he saw he invited Connolly down to see them play. A management contract was offered on the spot.

Connolly, nicknamed 'Father' Frank for his valuable 'parental' guidance of the fledgling outfit, may not have saved them from the rude awakening of eviction notices, but he certainly tried to arrange the band's chaotic affairs into some semblance of order, and ensured that they were kept busy for most of the following year, playing around the New Hampshire/New England/New York areas, honing their material and crafting their stage show.

Later, Aerosmith found themselves ensconced in Boston's Manchester Sheraton Hotel, where their new manager had booked rooms for rehearsal purposes, and they remained there for several months, working on some rough demos which Connolly could hawk around.

By this time, however, Connolly felt he needed assistance from a more knowledgeable rock 'n' roll manager. He was experienced in promoting and working with booking companies, but not in dealing with record companies. So he approached the New York management team of Steve Leber and David Krebs, a powerful pair of reputable impresarios who, he felt, could help take the band to the next stage of development. Thus, a deal was worked out with Leber and Krebs which would effectively hand the group over to them in return for a meaty slice of the pie, which included a cut of the band's publishing and a co-management credit for the first two albums.

The year was 1972 and the Leber-Krebs organisation immediately set about plotting Aerosmith's career with shrewd, business-minded efficiency. They wasted no time in sending a demo to Clive Davis, the president of Columbia Records, a subsidiary of the huge CBS corporation, and persuading him to check out their exciting new band at Max's Kansas City, the downtown rock club in Manhattan's Union Square where many undiscovered star acts had made their NY début.

Suitably intrigued, Clive Davis watched the gig with mounting interest, later squeezing into the tiny backstage area after the set to state, with an alarming sense of understatement, ''Yes, I think we can do something with you.''

Aerosmith, to their amazement, had landed a major recording deal, reportedly signing to Columbia in the summer of 1972 for a then-remarkable $125,000. More specifically, the band had signed to Leber-Krebs, who'd struck a very-profitable-thank-you production deal with Columbia, a situation which would aggravate the band's relationship with their management in years to come. But nonetheless, when David Krebs turned up just before one of their high school gigs with a fistful of CBS dollars and a recording contract demanding two albums a year, the five friends with stars in their eyes and holes in their shoes saw a chance to escape from the gutter that they weren't about to pass up.

Aerosmith's road to success, hindsight reveals, was now a 'One Way Street' . . .

CHAPTER THREE

ON A WING AND A PRAYER

AEROSMITH DIVEBOMBED into the butt-end of 1972 with the kind of euphoric anticipation normally reserved for pools winners awaiting their huge cardboard cheque from some dodgy desperate-for-work 'celebrity' who is famous for having once been famous. They may have been 'babes in the wood' in terms of experience, but they were fired with a kind of all-pervasive idealistic bluster which always suggested they weren't going to squander their CBS lifeline.

Moreover, while the band themselves were greener than a St. Patrick's Day parade, the Leber-Krebs management bedrock was well equipped for their stern paternal role. Lately their resolve had been tested by their experiences of managing The New York Dolls, the ill-fated glam-rock boy-wonders who counted David Johansen and Johnny Thunders (later to find success with The Heartbreakers) among their numbers. The pair had met whilst working in the New York offices of the William Morris Agency, a long-established and world famous booking agency which has turned many of its tea-boys into successful businessmen, and their enterprising outlook and intuitive sense of timing made them a powerful combination.

Steve Leber, the older, more conventional managerial character of the two, concentrated most of his efforts on The New York Dolls at this time, with Krebs – the younger, Jewish lawyer-type half of the partnership – assuming more responsibility for Aerosmith. And ironically it was The Dolls who were the golden boys of the age, precocious Big Apple punks at a time when New York was something of a New Wave Babylon, hailed by critics as monsters in the making. They looked ominous enough when they released their first album, 'New York Dolls', on the Mercury label in 1973 followed by the prophetically-titled 'Too Much Too Soon' in 1974, but a combination of self-destructive personalities and short-sighted decision-making precipitated their premature demise.

Before the downfall of The Dolls, however, Krebs remembers Aerosmith being "soooo jealous" of them. Clouded in hype, enormously hip

and glam-darlings of the New York set long before Kiss had raided their mothers' cosmetic bags, The Dolls commanded the attention of the media while Aerosmith slogged around the East Coast states in rickety station wagons, "Literally," according to Brad Whitford, "playing for our supper."

But times were a-changing for the eager young 'Smiths. With an albeit modest CBS budget in the coffers, the band set to work on their début album at the local Intermedia Sound recording studio with producer Adrian Barber, who'd previously worked with Cream, Vanilla Fudge, The Young Rascals and The Allman Brothers, quickly knocking into shape many of the numbers which had formed the basis of their live set.

"We were very excited to be actually making a record and thought it was really cool," Brad Whitford told the author more recently, "although now we realise how archaic all the equipment was! Somebody actually saved the very first mixing board we used on that album, and when I saw it some years later it looked like it was made of cardboard, with knobs the size of car headlamps!"

"They were real Stone Age studios," adds Tom Hamilton, "a real Frankenstein's lab of a place. But we'd been on the road for two years prior to going into the studios, so we'd played the songs many, many times and we were all fired up to lay them down as dynamically as possible."

The album did indeed sound very 'live', recorded in just two weeks and full of the kind of bar-room bravado and streetwise suss that had been ingrained in the band since Day One.

Just prior to the sessions Steven decided to change his surname to Tyler in order to avoid the constant mispronunciations. "I picked the name Tyler out of a hat," he explained later. "I knew

choose as the band's first stab at the singles chart: an epic of soul-searching emotion called 'Dream On', which harked back to the days when Tyler would tinker on his dad's grand piano in Sunapee, and which was arguably the first great power-ballad in US rock. From its very conception Tyler had a notion of its anthemic potential, but he could hardly have perceived the significance of one of its lines, as it would apply to the fluctuating fortunes of the band some 10 years later: 'You've got to lose to know how to win . . .'

Closing the first side was 'One Way Street', a jazzy, harmonica-streaked shuffle through girl problem territory, and then picking up the baton at the outset of the flick, 'Mama Kin', embellished by the wheezing sax-appeal of David Woodford, wrote another chapter of rock history with its swaggering gypsy cool, subsequently embedding itself in the band's live set for years to come and appearing not only on Guns n' Roses début EP 'Live ?!*@ 'Like A Suicide' . . . but also on Steven Tyler's left arm as a tattoo!

"I was just so proud of that tune," he explained later, "that I figured it would live forever one way or another – on my flesh if not in the record books!"

Tyler needn't have worried. 'Mama Kin' was one of the two classic originals on the album (along with 'Dream On', a minor hit on its first foray into US singledom, reaching number 59 later in 1973), although 'Write Me' remains irrepressible with its stomping 12-bar danceability, 'Movin' Out' (a tale of eviction from their humble Boston abode) retains its interest as Joe Perry's first compositional contribution on vinyl, and 'Walkin' The Dog' remains memorable if not for its delightfully down 'n' dirty groove, then certainly for Tyler's efforts on the wood flute!

Simply entitled 'Aerosmith' and fronted by a photograph of the band in lurid, hippy-ish clobber, surrounded by a cloudy, sky-type design – evidently a reflection of the band's 'spacey' name – the album hit the American record stores in January 1973 but wasn't issued in the UK until October 1974. On the back cover, local Boston journalist Stu Werbin scrawled an excited tribute to the band, recalling his introduction to Aerosmith through what was called 'The Weekly Boogie' at Boston University, and referring to the band's desire as Third Generation rockers to create something new as the 'Big Get Off'.

"Turn the volume up loud, roll back the carpet if you have one, and learn to dance," he wrote. The album was . . . "for the young, and the young in the head, and anybody who can still take it raw."

America's *Creem* magazine obviously could still take it raw. In its April 1974 edition 'Aerosmith' was given a definite thumbs-up: "They've got style up their ass," the review opined, "but never lose touch with the five o'clock shadow pushiness that is as much a part of rock as dummy spots and bubble skirts were a part of the fifties street

Above: A young Tyler keeps it under his hat.
Below left: The influential New York Dolls who shared Aerosmith's management.
Below: The cover of Aerosmith's eponymous debut album.

what I was experiencing on-stage was stardom, so I thought of myself as a different name." He wrote five out of the eight tracks himself; two were co-written by him, one with Joe Perry ('Movin' Out'), the other with an old roadie friend from Yonkers days, Steven Emspack ('Somebody'). And that left just one cover on the record, a rough 'n' tumble run-through of the 1963 Rufus Thomas chestnut 'Walkin' The Dog' which The Rolling Stones covered on their first LP.

'Make It' got the ball rolling though, an intimate reflection of Tyler's heart-on-sleeve clamour for recognition which began with the fitting opening line of 'Good evening people, welcome to the show . . .', and went on to extol the virtues of 'paying your dues' in its urgent plea to 'Make it, don't break it . . .' Simple, high-spirited R&B-soaked rock 'n' roll, it set the tone and indeed the standard for what was to follow on a formative, yet ruggedly recommendable début.

'Somebody' was next, moulded from a primitive rock formula and including a Joe Perry solo mimicked by Steven Tyler's voice, a gimmick being made famous in the parallel universe of Deep Purple by Ritchie Blackmore and Ian Gillan. And then came the song that Columbia would

cosmology. Sure you'll hear influences, some quite obvious at that, but we all had to suck somebody's tit, and whatta buncha tits these chubby-lipped delinquents have gone after! For starters, they learned a few chords from Rory Gallagher's Taste days. 'Nuff said?''

Less passionate reviewers, however, dismissed the record as little more than garbage, and the band as second rate Rolling Stones impersonators.

The group were stung hard by the negative reviews, not least because deep down they knew they were true: Tyler was a ringer for Jagger, and the resemblance had more to do with a touch of hero-worship cloning than merely genetic coincidence, and Perry had modelled his bad-boy broodiness on the studied fag-in-the-corner-of-the-mouth posing of Keith Richards, to the point where even years later roadies would joke that whenever Perry went missing on tour he was probably only in his hotel room brushing up on his Keith Richards routine.

Nevertheless, the band were determined to stick to their guns whatever the press said about them. They did look like The Stones, but they weren't going to make a conscious effort to change the way they looked. And in any case, musically they always saw themselves more along the lines of The Yardbirds, Cream and Led Zeppelin. They were fascinated by all the great British bands like The Yardbirds who sounded so classy and powerful, and they made no bones about the fact that they wanted to be the first American band to compete on that same level.

"In my mind the hardest, ballsiest rock band that ever came out of America was Aerosmith."

W. AXL ROSE, GUNS N' ROSES

The first signs that Aerosmith might just make the grade came when 'Dream On' began to get regular plays on local radio stations. The song had topped the request list first at the WVBF FM station, and then later at almost all the Boston stations, and Columbia had eventually responded by remixing and releasing it as a single in June, with 'Somebody' on the B-side. As it began to move up the charts in over 30 areas of the country, its haunting refrain took a new significance for its authors: 'Dream on . . . dream until your dreams come true . . .'

Exasperatingly though, during that summer of 1973 Columbia became embroiled in payola allegations which ultimately led to the departure of its President, Clive Davis. With a new régime taking over the company, Aerosmith's standing in priority terms inevitably sank. The new decision makers seemed reluctant to put themselves out for their former boss' protégés, and 'Dream On' failed to realise its full potential in the national chart.

Nevertheless, with 'Aerosmith' becoming the biggest selling album within a 50-mile radius of Boston for the rest of that year, the band hit the road once again in an effort to impose themselves on a more widespread audience simply through their constant availability.

''It wasn't like Led Zeppelin were out there on the road in America all the time,'' Perry explained later, ''and The Stones weren't always coming to your town. We were the guys you could actually see.''

And so they sweated it out in the clubs and colleges, grabbing support slots with 'name' bands whenever they could, and staging their own little headliners whenever they couldn't. The Kinks played host to Aerosmith during the summer of 1973, as did Mott The Hoople, then riding high on the back of their classic hit single 'All The Young Dudes' from the year before. Krebs had considered landing that tour as a major coup, ensuring as it did that Aerosmith would be playing in front of 2500 – 3000 people a night in halls such as California's Santa Monica Civic, instead of 300 – 500 capacity clubs in obscure Midwest backwaters.

But there were plenty of small theatre gigs to trudge through as well, including the Electric Ballroom in Atlanta, Georgia, where Aerosmith opened for a young, acid-headed British band on their third tour of the States to promote their 'Space Ritual' album: Hawkwind.

"We'd played with a lot of good bands on that tour," recalls Lemmy, the Motorhead mainman who served his apprenticeship with Dave Brock's crackpot cosmic crew. "UFO, Rush, Frank Marino . . . and Aerosmith, mainly I suppose because Leber and Krebs used to manage us in America and they figured they'd kill two bands with one stone! Neither of us had any kind of following in those days, and I remember Aerosmith being very nervy and untogether. Steven Tyler didn't have his

stage persona worked out then – no scarves around the microphone or anything. But even in those days you could tell they had something going for them."

One of the things they had going for them was a management team whose strategy was to pair them deliberately with any 'dinosaur' band on the road, thus making the younger outfit look all the more youthful and exciting. And in one of the more memorable mismatches since Jimi Hendrix supported The Monkees, Aerosmith found themselves opening a number of dates for the extremely weird and progressive Mahavishnu Orchestra, the band led by cult guitar-God John McLaughlin, which also featured renowned jazz-rock drummer Billy Cobham (soon to forge a noted solo career) and keyboard wizard Jan Hammer, who more recently wrote the theme tune to the *Miami Vice* TV series! The Mahavishnus liked to meditate on stage before their shows and McLaughlin would demand a minute's silence from the audience after Aerosmith's set, to 'cool the vibes', and prepare everyone's mental state for his music. But Tom Hamilton has always maintained the audience needed the rest!

For Aerosmith there was no time to rest, not even when they came off stage. The kids may have gone wild during the band's set, but afterwards they'd slope back to their humdrum, predictable working class existences. The band,

Thus, Aerosmith adopted a habit which would dog their career for a painful, unlucky-for-some 13 years. Yet as toxic levels increased steadily, so did the band's profile as gruelling roadwork began to establish a sizeable following on the East Coast. But that didn't ease any of the record company pressure which demanded that their next album perform a lot better commercially than its predecessor, and the band sensed it was make-or-break time.

* * *

This was very much on Aerosmith's collective mind as they set to work on their second album in the autumn of 1973. New York's Record Plant studios were chosen as the venue – used by The Rolling Stones and Led Zeppelin among others and thus hallowed territory as far as Aerosmith were concerned – with producers Jack Douglas and Ray Colcord working under the guidance of 'Executive Producer' Bob Ezrin, who'd spent the early seventies making a name for the Nimbus 9 organisation by producing a batch of Alice Cooper albums, including 'Love It To Death' (1971), 'Killer' (1972), 'School's Out' (1972) and 'Billion Dollar Babies' (1973) – the latter, incidentally, engineered by Douglas, who himself went on to produce Alice's 'Muscle Of Love' LP in 1974.

Interestingly though, while Ezrin emerged as one of the top producers of the seventies and eighties, working with the likes of Kiss, Lou Reed, Pink Floyd and Hanoi Rocks, it was Aerosmith's relationship with Jack Douglas which was to prove the most significant. He'd first worked for the Leber-Krebs team when he engineered The New York Dolls' début album, but there was something special about his working relationship with Aerosmith. From the very beginning there was a creative spark between the two parties, with Tom Hamilton admitting afterwards that it was Douglas' skill with arrangements which helped take the quality of the material onto a different level. And over the following five years the combination would concoct some of the finest rock sounds ever to escape from America.

For their first album together though, Aerosmith and Douglas concentrated on capturing the band's established live sound and embellishing it with a smattering of sophistication, ensuring a slightly more polished and progressive album than 'Aerosmith'. Once again Tyler had a hand in all of the record's original compositions, with the only

meanwhile, would simply go backstage and get even higher. In reference to the Mahavishnu dates, Tom Hamilton told *Rolling Stone* magazine, ''We weren't really into meditating, we'd already found our own ways to meditate, chemically.'' And it was true that even at this early stage in their career Aerosmith had begun to slip into the dangerous, ever-deepening rut of drug abuse.

''The 'head' we were in never stopped,'' explained Tyler. ''I had to do as much cocaine as I could, and I had to drink as much as I could. I had to keep that buzz going. I thought I had to be in that buzz – that warm, little, safe place – all the time. It never stopped. We brought the party with us wherever we went.''

For a young band in the early seventies struggling to emulate their sixties heroes, taking drugs ''just came natural'' to impressionable souls like Steven Tyler. Getting high was what it was all about, as that was what 'real' rock 'n' rollers from The Stones to The Who and Cream to Jimi Hendrix did. And as Tyler himself remembers from as long ago as his days with The Strangeurs, ''If you didn't do all the drugs you had, you just weren't cool.''

cover this time being the 1951 Tim Bradshaw/Lois Mann/Howie Kay tale of love on a locomotive, 'Train Kept A Rollin'', which had come to the attention of Tyler via The Yardbirds, who'd recorded their variation of the age-old blues standard for their 'Having A Rave-Up With The Yardbirds' LP in 1966.

The album kicked off with 'Same Old Song And Dance', a Tyler/Perry tune awash with sassy, brass-injected dancefloor dynamics, wrapped around a loose storyline of a loser caught up in murder. Then came 'Lord Of The Thighs', Tyler's tongue-in-cheek skit on William Golding's classic novel *Lord Of The Flies* which, as you'd expect, had nothing whatsoever to do with precocious brats marooned on a desert island! The song was actually inspired by some of the more alluring denizens in the neighbourhood around the Ramada Inn on New York's 48th Street and 8th Avenue, where Aerosmith stayed during the recording of the album.

Tyler and Perry's sixties-sounding 'Spaced', however, remains one of the more obscure 'Smith cuts, as does 'Woman Of The World', another song from Tyler's writing days with Don Soloman. The former, featuring co-producer Ray Colcord on keyboards, recounted Tyler's fear of a lonely post-holocaust life on another planet, while the latter, a fairly standard lust song acoustically-combed by Perry's 12-string, featured a mid-section guitar riff stolen from Fleetwood Mac's 'Rattlesnake Shake', and which would crop up three years later during the fading moments of 'Rats In The Cellar' on 'Rocks'. Neither shook the world, and both still sound the most dated songs on the record even today.

'S.O.S. (Too Bad)', meanwhile, found the band opening side two on top form, with Perry's rusty-razor riff and Tyler's half-sneering vocal wails urging the track along. And then 'Train Kept A Rollin'', complete with its uptempo 'live' coda, started a trend that was to open the floodgates for a thousand concert encores in years to come.

Next came the hauntingly exquisite ballad 'Seasons Of Wither', one of Tyler's most emotive achievements to date, written during a bleak December night of solitude in the old Boston apartment, and a statement of maturity among the nudge-nudge boys' room banter of tracks like 'Lord Of The Thighs'. And finally, 'Pandora's Box' – Joey Kramer's only writing credit in 'Smith history – brought the record to a climax with more brassy brilliance and sex-on-the-brain sentiments. The end result was a far more instant and cohesive record, hinting firmly at the vinyl glories just around the corner.

The whole package surfaced in February 1974 (November 1974 in Britain) under the title of 'Get Your Wings'. Originally it was to be called 'A Night In The Ruts', as Tyler had suggested when introducing new songs like 'Pandora's Box' and 'Train Kept A Rollin'' during concerts. But luckily for the band 'Get Your Wings' stuck and inspired the first incarnation of the band's now-famous 'wings' logo.

Sadly, on its first album sleeve appearance it

looked more like the 'Batman' logo, with a huge furry-looking 'A' hovering above an immensely boring black and white photograph of the band. But it bore no relation to the quality of the record itself, which proved to the band and their fans, if not their critics, that they were moving forward in leaps and bounds. Fittingly, the album became the top-selling album in Greater Boston within weeks of its release, locking itself into the middle region of the US charts and consistently selling between 5000 – 6,000 copies a week. And the first single from the album, 'Same Old Song And Dance' – released in March with 'Pandora's Box' on the flip – dominated all the major FM airwaves, doing well enough to appease any doubters among the Columbia ranks.

By March Aerosmith were on the road in the States again, supporting Deep Purple (on their first tour with new members Glenn Hughes and David Coverdale) at the New Haven Coliseum in Connecticut on March 14 – a bill opened by Elf, the forerunner of Ritchie Blackmore's Rainbow, featuring vocalist Ronnie James Dio – and then grafting throughout the year wherever and whenever they could, especially around the North-Eastern states like Michigan and Massachusetts, where their popularity meant they could comfortably play two consecutive nights in some venues. They may still have had to open the bill at arenas like New York's Madison Square Garden for big bands like Britain's Black Sabbath (a gig where then-Sabbath singer Ozzy Osbourne remembers them going down ''an absolute storm''), but they could headline in places like New England, where some fans found Blue Oyster Cult opening the show.

The band's set at this time would generally open with 'S.O.S.' (which according to Tom stood for 'Same Old Shit'), lurching straight into 'Somebody' and then recalling 'Write Me', 'Walkin' The Dog', 'One Way Street', 'Mama Kin' and 'Dream On' from the first album, as well as showcasing new nuggets like 'Lord Of The Thighs', 'Same Old Song And Dance', 'Pandora's Box' and 'Woman Of The World', which the band rounded off with a passage they later fitted into the finale of 'Rats In The Cellar'.

Lastly, the 'Smiths would usually sign off with 'Train Kept A Rollin'', the second single from the album which was released in America during September (with 'Spaced' on the B-side; the crowd noises having been strangely erased). It was a simple but solid show, Tyler naturally hogging the spotlight with his outrageous outfits and new habit of tying scarves around his microphone stand, and the band attracted a lot of positive press, particularly in *Creem* where one journalist even stuck his neck out to the extent of suggesting the band were ''well on the way to becoming a big group nationally.''

The band's train was certainly a-rolling by now, the question was: was it on the right track?

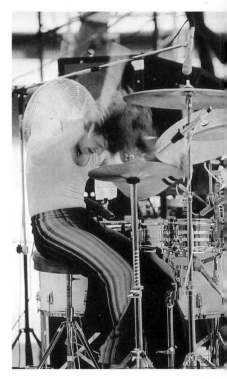

CHAPTER FOUR

AMERICA ROCKS

AS 1975 DAWNED, MANY OF the world's top heavy rock bands were in the process of etching personal paragraphs into the annals of the genre's history, moving through what retrospection deems 'classic' eras.

To put the year into some sort of chronological perspective, 1975 was when Led Zeppelin released 'Physical Graffiti', Tommy Bolin replaced Rainbow-bound Ritchie Blackmore in Deep Purple, Black Sabbath released their 'Sabotage' album, and Queen had 'Bohemian Rhapsody' at number one in the UK singles charts for a staggering nine weeks.

In America, meanwhile, Peter Frampton came alive with his record-breaking double live set, Kiss definitely looked like they were 'Dressed To Kill' as they also released a double live package entitled 'Alive!', ZZ Top danced a crazed 'Fandango' and Bachman Turner Overdrive started the year by proclaiming in the singles charts on both sides of the Atlantic, 'You Ain't Seen Nothin' Yet'.

For Aerosmith that very title would have had a special, almost prophetic meaning, as 1975 was to be the year that the adopted Bostonians would expand their pocket of North-East support to incorporate the whole of America, picking up gold discs for both 'Aerosmith' and 'Get Your Wings' to signify 500,000 sales in the States as their third album, 'Toys In The Attic', stormed into the US charts, going gold within four months, turning platinum (1,000,000 sales) by the end of the year and sticking on the chart for over two years solid. Such was the impact both socially and psychologically on a nation of budding rock musicians, that things would never be the same again for the American hard rock scene.

'Toys In The Attic' was recorded at the Record Plant in New York during the early months of 1975 and bore many familiar features. Once again Jack Douglas handled the production; once again Steven Tyler co-wrote all the originals on the record, reviving yet another of his songs with his Chain Reaction partner Don Soloman in 'You See Me Crying', continuing the trend set on the band's first two LPs; and once again there was a golden oldie dusted down and dressed up in 'Smith rags, this time Fred Weismantel's 1952 tongue-in-cheek bopper, 'Big Ten Inch Record'.

But 'Toys . . .' was different in that it was the first 'Smith record to have a title track (and there have only been four in the band's 11 studio LPs to date); and, more importantly, it was the first album which really focused the band's manic, frayed-at-the-edges live sound into something tangible on vinyl, capturing a spirit which at this point was fired by certain toxic excesses rather than dampened by it.

In keeping with the band's rather kaleidoscopic state of mind, the title track opened the floodgates with a full-pelt clash of screaming guitars and nightmarish lyrical imagery, recalling strange childhood dreams. Undoubtedly the finest Tyler/Perry composition thus far, 'Toys In The Attic' would become a catalyst for the aspirations of an endless stream of American hard rock wannabes, setting a standard few, if any, have exceeded since, crystallising as it did the classic vision of a rock band in full flight. It remains in Aerosmith's live set to this day.

Sadly though, Tyler and Hamilton's 'Uncle Salty' (with Hamilton on rhythm guitar) paled into insignificance beside it, droning on about a poor orphan girl's desperate plight after getting mixed up in drugs and prostitution in a morbid manner reminiscent of The Beatles at their most depressing. But 'Adam's Apple' (including the line, 'She ate it, knowing it was love at first bite', with 'Love At First Bite' originally being considered as the album's title) soon restored sanity with a twin-lead guitar groove good enough to allow Tyler to get away with his rather ridiculous adaptation of the Adam and Eve episode without sounding like some Biblical buffoon. And then came another Tyler masterstroke in the shape of 'Walk This Way', a high school boogie through the adolescent assault course of losing your virginity, soon to hit the upper echelons of the US singles chart on its way to becoming one of the band's best-loved songs ever.

"That song started out as just a Joe Perry lick and then I put my rhythmic lyrics that stem from my days as a drummer over the top of that," Tyler told *RAW* magazine. "I remember making up those lyrics the night we were meant to record the vocals. I wrote them on the walls of the Record Plant stairway! When I listen to that song now it's so raw you can tell I wrote those lyrics on the spot!"

With the saucy, groin-level innuendo of the bold and brassy 'Big Ten Inch Record' bringing side one to a close in a hail of honky-tonk piano and harmonica (courtesy of session specialist Scott Cushnie and Steven Tyler respectively), the second side kicked into gear with another future

classic, 'Sweet Emotion'. The tale of a teenage Lolita flashing her flesh at a 'Smith show, penned by Tyler and Hamilton, the track built from an innocent doodle on the bass guitar into one of the band's most off-the-wall hard rockers, lurching disjointedly into several different sections and yet somehow remaining strangely cohesive. Its record company seal of approval came when it was chosen as the album's first single, backed by 'Uncle Salty' and released almost simultaneously with the album in April. Its public seal of approval can still be monitored by its welcome presence in the band's set 15 years on.

Yet while musically Aerosmith's creativity was beginning to hit a few peaks, mentally their gruelling tour-album-tour-album-tour schedule was beginning to take its toll, a state of affairs duly reflected in the seriously anaemic faces on the photo on the back cover. 'No More No More', another Tyler/Perry raunchy R&B special, even had the singer complaining, 'Blood stains the ivories of my daddy's baby grand/Ain't seen the daylight since we started this band,' concluding with ironic perception, 'Times are a-changing, nothing ever stands still/If I don't start changing, I'll be writing my will.' It was the first vinyl admission of the kamikaze lifestyle which was starting to chip away at the stone of Aerosmith's achievements.

Nevertheless, with the booming Zeppelin-ish

groan of 'Round And Round' (Brad Whitford's first writing credit) and the epic, orchestral weepie 'You See Me Crying' polishing proceedings off in a pile-up of violins and sodden hankies, 'Toys In The Attic' was certified a bona fide US rock triumph, at last earning the band some positive reviews both in America and across the pond in Britain, where rock fans spoilt by having the likes of The Stones, The Who, Zeppelin, Purple, Sabbath, Yes, Genesis and most of the other 'classic' outfits of the day on their doorstep, were becoming aware of the rumblings of a number of newcomers Stateside.

"'Toys In The Attic' is the slickest thing they've ever attempted," wrote *Creem* magazine in August, "and will no doubt take a deserved place in the Rock Hall Of Fame – it's an invocation to all our demon brothers. When it's nasty, it's a musical slaughterhouse; when it's sensuous, it's like doin' the do to your puderoo in a blendful of mushy artichoke hearts . . ."

Ultimately, the reviewer reckoned, it showed the band maturing as musicians, "while maintaining their standing as promoters of the punk ethic," capturing the band performing "with a pythonic

"I don't know how I missed them in the seventies, but I've since made a point of getting all their albums. I think they're a fabulous band."
DAVID COVERDALE, WHITESNAKE

TWENTY THREE

Right: Tyler at the Record Plant Studios in New York.
Far right: Management stablemate and regular support act Ted Nugent.
Below: America's *Creem* magazine gives 'Toys In The Attic' the thumbs up.

ditty called "Tennessee Walker" are the only minor flaws. The Beau Brummels are just as good in 1975 as they were in '65, and in their case that's saying plenty.

Ken Barnes

AEROSMITH
Toys in the Attic
(Columbia)

Under the production of Jack Douglas, Stevie Tyler and company have in their third album finally matured as musicians, while maintaining their standing as promoters of the punk ethic. Aerosmith perform with a pythonic grace that's born outa playing second and third fiddle to such hoary rockers as Mott and the Dolls. When they surge out into the void with a song it's an expression of a certain kind of frustration: the essence of a soused punknacity created solely to keep the depths of boredom company. *Toys in the Attic* is the slickest thing they've ever attempted and will no doubt take a deserved place in the Rock Hall of Fame—it's an invocation to all our demon brothers. When it's nasty, it's a musical slaughterhouse; when it's sensuous, it's like doin' the do to your puderoo in a blender full of mushy artichoke hearts—ohhh, bay-bee!

While there are a few weak spots on the record, only two stand out: "Big Ten Inch Record" is a throwaway break song, and "You See Me Crying" just isn't given enough time to completely realize itself. The rest ranges from the thundering "Round and Round," with its rolling bass lines and crystalline, sky-slicing guitar passages, to the grey backbeat ballad "Sweet Emotion" and the pugnacious punkitude of the title track. What with the passing of the Lords, all hail the New Creatures; you see, Jim did know what he was talking about.

Joe Fernbacher

grace that's born out of playing second and third fiddle to such hoary old rockers as Mott and The Dolls.'' It was thumbs up all round.

Indeed, as 'Toys . . .' made Aerosmith Columbia's top-selling artist by the end of 1975, eclipsing even Barbra Streisand, Bob Dylan and Bruce Springsteen, contemporaries like ZZ Top, Blue Oyster Cult, Black Oak Arkansas and Kiss were all beginning to earn reputations in Europe as Bands To Watch, with hot, promising new talent like REO Speedwagon, Styx, Cheap Trick and Ted Nugent not too far behind. So highly was Nugent rated that Leber and Krebs swiftly took charge of his management affairs, thus ploughing the former Amboy Duke and self-styled Detroit City madman's career into a furrow parallel to Aerosmith's, and ensuring many an Aerosmith/Nugent double bill in future.

But for the time being Aerosmith were potentially the brightest of all the Stateside starlets, encouraging UK commentators like *Sounds*' Geoff Barton to record that, '''Toys In The Attic' is a good, healthy, unpretentious powerpack album, showing Aerosmith at their very best.''

''We really did put everything we had into that record ('Toys . . .'),'' Tom Hamilton told the author while in a reflective mood a couple of years ago, ''and I guess the reason why it turned out so well was because we had the perfect combination of great songs and the kind of 'fired up' spirit that you get after a lot of touring. We were like a well-oiled machine at that time and had lots of dynamite songs that we couldn't wait to get down on tape. So no wonder the album came out sounding like it did!''

''Yeah, we were getting used to working in the studio,'' said Perry. ''The shock of being in the Record Plant had worn off, and we were getting into our own way of working with Jack Douglas. It was just an exciting time.''

Barely was the record finished, however, than Aerosmith were treading the boards once more, obliging the Krebs business ethic of 'work work work' and sewing up each territory one by one with a recurring blitz of live dates. When 'Toys . . .' appeared in April the band (plus keyboard sidekick Cushnie) were working their way across Ohio, with dates in Toledo and Cleveland on April 11 and 12 respectively, then came the now obligatory double-header in Boston, followed by riots in Syracuse, Providence, Augusta, Baltimore, Grand Rapids and Dayton. The month ended with a three-night stint at the Cobo Hall in Detroit, a stronghold for the band which now almost doubled as a home-from-home.

June found the Beantown boys spreading their wings a little further afield. They began the month with shows in Evansville and Indianapolis in the state of Indiana, edging through the unfamiliar

territory of Minnesota, North Dakota, Wisconsin, Missouri, Colorado, California and Arizona, before venturing out to the Hawaiian island of Honolulu on July 13 for a date at the HIC Arena. By the autumn, when they'd returned to their backyard in the North East, Aerosmith were well on the way to national fame.

The nationwide network of AM radio stations in America at this point had also begun to take notice of the mushrooming Aerosmith phenomenon and a string of singles were released in the hope of extra promotion: 'Walk This Way' (backed by 'Round And Round') crept out in August, 'You See Me Crying' (coupled with 'Toys In The Attic') in November, and finally 'Dream On', almost three-years-old now, was re-released in December in a stroke of super-shrewd timing. The radio stations played it to death, it was on juke boxes throughout the land, and brainwashed and already-converted fans bought it in their tens of thousands. By the beginning of 1976 the song had reached number six on the US singles chart, effectively sealing Aerosmith's destiny as America's hottest rock 'n' roll property of the mid-seventies.

* * *

Flushed with the success of 'Dream On', Aerosmith ploughed into the task of recording their fourth album with renewed relish. Original ideas were recorded at their hideout, The Wherehouse in Waltham, Massachusetts – Aerosmith World Headquarters to those who worked for the band – and then it was back to their old stomping ground of the Record Plant in New York City with Jack Douglas taking his now customary position behind the desk and Jay Messina once again helping out as engineer.

The result, unleashed on an eager American nation in May 1976, was what many observers, the author included, still consider to be Aerosmith's finest hour: 'Rocks'.

Quite simply, if 'Toys In The Attic' defined Aerosmith's sound, then 'Rocks' *perfected* it. 'Rocks' was quintessential Aerosmith, a spine-tingling *tour de force* of sleaze-ridden songs and powerhouse production, lashing low-slung guitar licks and gum-chewing, gutter-level lyrics on rampant, rumbustious rhythms without losing sight of any melodic sensibilities. A true classic of its kind.

The hit list went as follows:

'Back In The Saddle' – a time-honoured Tyler/Perry rodeo romp through cowboy country, inevitably ending with Tyler 'Peeling off my boots and chaps' and hitting the sack with some wanton Western wench while Perry delivers some tortuous lead lines. A regular concert opener in years to come.

'Last Child' – fearsome funk from Brad Whitford over Tyler's rap-like lyrical longing to go 'home sweet home' where, apparently, you 'can't catch no dose from a hot-tail poon-tang sweetheart who could make a silk purse from J. Paul Get and his ear – with her face in her beer!' Quite . . .

'Rats In The Cellar' – hurtling hard rock from the blossoming Tyler/Perry partnership, spewing

the band heard about the San Andreas fault. Some great 'wah-wah' guitar lines, too.

'Get The Lead Out' – more heavy, hip-swinging funk straight from the dancefloor of some dodgy, downtown New York nightclub, coated with enough sleaze to please.

'Lick And A Promise' – high-energy, stadium-strutting rock 'n' roll bursting with unbelievable exuberance. Like 'Get The Lead Out', written by Tyler and Perry and a sizzling slice of Aerosmith at their very best.

'Home Tonight' – Tyler's tearful ballad, enhanced by a 101-piece orchestra, and crowned by one of the sweetest Joe Perry solos on record.

The whole bone-crushing caboodle came wrapped in a jet-black sleeve with five diamonds across the front (another effort by the Pacific Eye And Ear design company, who were also responsible for the surreal cartoon on the front cover of 'Toys . . .'), and was dedicated to the memories of Joe Perry's father, Anthony D. Perry, and Herb Spar, a close friend of the band, both of whom had passed away recently.

The record went platinum immediately upon release, swiftly passing the double platinum mark (2,000,000 sales), and fans and critics alike hailed it as the band's most sophisticated and consistent release so far, a classic American rock album.

''Two-thirds of the album,'' said the crucial

"They're the coolest bunch of mothers on the planet. They're incapable of making a bad record!"

TED NUGENT

sentiments of disgust at being down and out in New York. Owing much to Fleetwood Mac's 'Rattlesnake Shake' (a fact begrudgingly admitted by Tyler years later!), 'Rats . . .' was the natural successor to 'Toys In The Attic' as the band's most manic, full-pelt rocker, storming to a glorious guitar-slashed climax.

'Combination' – Joe Perry's first solo composition and a sullen, brooding beast of a track that's difficult to decipher. Weird lyrics, strange melody lines, a hauntingly distorted chorus and a chaotic, swirling finale that screeches to an unexpected halt. An appropriate musical extension of the moody persona Perry was beginning to cultivate.

'Sick As A Dog' – as cool and raunchy as they come, slipping and sliding along an irresistible Tom Hamilton-inspired good-time groove. (Note: This track ended up like an instrumental free-for-all, with Hamilton taking over on guitar while both Perry and Tyler added bass lines!)

'Nobody's Fault' – forged from a grinding, Sumo-heavy riff that rumbles along on Joey Kramer's hefty hi-hat shuffle, it featured one of Tyler's more serious lyrics, based on a news story

Creem review in the States, ''drives, thunders, shrills and crashes in at the top of its league. Joe Perry and Brad Whitford may be the best duel-guitar act running today – in 'Rats In The Cellar' they've finally managed to pull off a perfect Yardbirds steal, which makes them better than present day Led Zeppelin at dynamic tension, and in 'Combination' they pull out all the stops for a distortion war that, like all the best rave-ups, threatens to drown the whole track in the wrong kind of chaos, but manages to keep things just this side of Gehenna.''

Years later a whole new generation of American rock stars, including Slash from Guns n' Roses and Nikki Sixx from Motley Crue, were to cite 'Rocks' as one of the most influential albums of their youth, and on reflection even the ever-modest Tom Hamilton admitted it was the band's finest hour.

''It was the sequel to 'Toys In The Attic', and as such was really just a case of 'more of the same','' he explained, ''except that it was harder, more exotic and a little more specialised. We were really

contemporaries in expanding their huge domestic following on an international scale, their appetite for destruction was such that their management considered foreign travel an extremely dangerous proposition.

"Basically," Tyler explained later, "we never left the States because we were afraid to go through Customs. Hiding the stuff under band aids and inside backstage passes wasn't working any more. Our managers knew what sorta state we were in so what was the percentage for them in us going to Europe when they figured they'd end up having to bail us out?"

So when Aerosmith hit the road to do the rather pointless job of promoting 'Rocks' during the summer of 1976, it was the Stateside stadia which once again played host. Not that this bothered the band's management. *Circus Raves* magazine in America had published statistics the previous year showing Aerosmith to be one of the highest-earners on the US rock circuit, grossing $500,000 dollars in 26 gigs alone. Ahead of them in commercial terms were only megabands like Led Zeppelin, Alice Cooper, Jethro Tull and Rod Stewart And The Faces.

Aerosmith's amazing pulling power was highlighted no better than at the Pontiac Stadium in Detroit during May. 45,000 tickets were sold the first day they went on sale, and the band ended up selling out the 80,000 allocation at $10 each, leaving even the worst mathematician able to reach a final grossing figure of $800,000. Support act Foghat might have claimed to have drawn some proportion of that total from their own healthy Detroit following, but Aerosmith's mushrooming popularity was nonetheless undeniable.

In July *Circus* magazine set the tone for the rest of the summer with an editorial firework display in honour of America's new heroes. "Riding on the success of 'Rocks' they'll begin a two-and-a-half month supertour which will have them headlining in halls of 10,000 seats and up," it announced with patriotic pride. "Plus, they'll be playing about 25 major stadiums in cities like Boston, Philadelphia, Cleveland, Chicago, Los Angeles, San Francisco and Honolulu . . . with the group moving from east to west as the summer wanes." It was what every American kid wanted to hear, especially as Zeppelin were grounded following Robert Plant's car crash in Greece, and a US tour from The Stones was still in some doubt. While the cats are away . . .

However, with European media and public alike picking up on the soaraway success of Aerosmith in America, the Leber-Krebs think-tank began seriously contemplating the band's first visit to Europe during the long hot summer of 1976. The band wanted it, as England was as far as they were concerned the 'home of rock 'n' roll', and they'd always wanted to play in the backyard of their boyhood idols. And CBS, the band's European label, were also keen to have them come over and promote their back catalogue ('Aerosmith' having shifted only 900 copies in the UK at this time, 'Get Your Wings' even less). But

at our peak at the time."

And so they were . . . although all that meant was the only way for the band to go now was down. On the face of it the band had everything – high profile, hit records, huge mansions in the countryside around Boston and six-figured bank accounts. But beneath the surface their personal habits were starting to become destructive.

Joe Perry began shooting heroin during the recording of 'Rocks', Tyler was already on it, having progressed from pot, barbiturates, cocaine, acid, tuinols, seconals, black beauties, crystal methadrine, DMTs, STPs and just about anything else that had a drastic effect on mind and body. The other three, whilst also nursing personal chemical preferences, drank heavily.

Indeed, at a time when Aerosmith should have been hot on the heels of their hard rock

Leber and Krebs weren't so sure of the financial viabilities of lugging tons and tons of equipment halfway around the world to play tiny theatres, when the massive concert venues at home generated such a healthy revenue.

Nevertheless, a European tour was planned for the autumn of 1976 – originally a double-headlining package with Ted Nugent – and Hawkwind's manager, Doug Smith, was recruited as Aerosmith's European management representative, returning the favour that Leber-Krebs had bestowed upon Hawkwind in the States.

"I thought the idea of bringing Nugent and Aerosmith in together was crazy," Doug recalls, "because at this time I thought both bands had created a big enough aura of their own. So Nugent came first, during the autumn with the George Hatcher Band supporting, and he went down really well. But the big one was always going to be Aerosmith, because they'd built up this awesome reputation in America."

So before the band arrived in England the London office of CBS met to discuss advance promotion for Aerosmith's visit. They were under extra pressure because less than a year earlier CBS had been involved in the farcical events surrounding Bruce Springsteen's first visit to the UK for which they had coined the slogan 'At last . . . London is ready for Bruce Springsteen.' The hype backfired, Springsteen was furious and CBS's London office was held responsible. It was therefore crucial that the same thing didn't happen again with another prestige US act.

Their idea for Aerosmith, according to Doug Smith, was to utilise the subtle art of subliminal advertising – getting the band's name known without plastering it all over the place – and to this end Smith hatched a plan with CBS label manager Peter Evans to take Aerosmith into the unlikely world of boxing.

"There was a major fight in Britain just before the band were due to tour," explains Doug, "which was going to be shown on TV both sides of the Atlantic on the *World Of Sport* programme. Incredible as it may seem, we managed to get 'Aerosmith' printed down the side of the boxers' trunks, and consequently the name was flashed all around the world in one go! It was a real coup.

"The day after the fight Krebs phoned me in a panic. 'Douglas, there's a boxing promoter in Britain called Aerosmith! What are we going to do?' I couldn't help laughing when I broke the news to him the whole thing was a publicity stunt. He was amazed!"

With the promotional machinery now in full swing, Aerosmith's PR company in the UK, Heavy Publicity, started looking for ways of getting the band coverage in the all important British music press which, spoilt by the dominance enjoyed by UK rock acts during the previous decade, tended to look upon American rock bands with some scorn. In charge of the company, which also provided PR for the likes of Black Sabbath, Mann, Sassafrass, Ted Nugent, REO Speedwagon, Styx, Kansas and Black Oak Arkansas, was

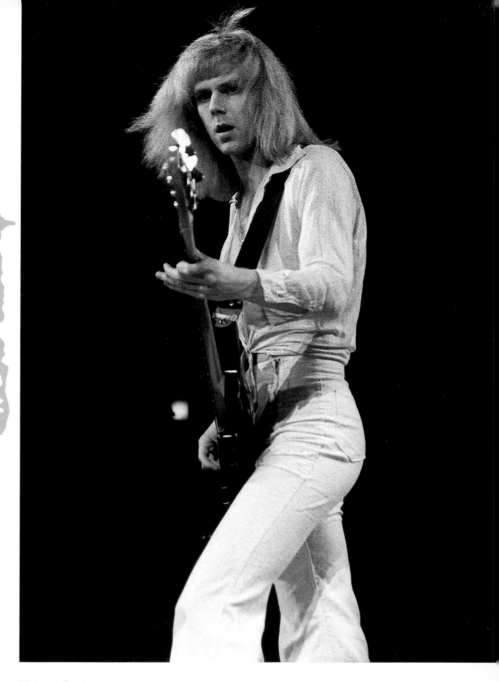

Richard Ogden.

"What we really wanted for the band was a few front covers in the music press," says Ogden, who after an illustrious career at various record companies now handles Paul McCartney's business affairs. "So I took Chris Welch from *Melody Maker* over to America to interview Steven Tyler. It turned out to be one of the strangest experiences of my life. We flew to Boston, were taken by private plane (by President Kennedy's former pilot!) to New Hampshire where Tyler lived, we landed in the middle of this golf course and the first thing we saw was Bobby Womack (another Leber-Krebs act) sitting on this park bench in a huge white fur coat smoking a joint. We thought then things were a bit odd, but then we found ourselves hanging around in Tyler's house for two days because he wouldn't speak to us! He was

"I've been a fan since their first single ('Dream On'). We've played with them four times and I think they're incredible. They're the best rock band on earth at the moment. They've influenced so many rock bands over the years, but now they're better than ever."

RUDOLPH SCHENKER, SCORPIONS

TWENTY SEVEN

actually in the house as well but he couldn't be found – he was hiding from us, entirely on his own, in a huge empty building that had no furniture in it or anything. It was all very strange.''

''Eventually I did get to interview him,'' Welch continues the story, ''and not only that but he took me for a spin in his Porsche, whipped me across Lake Sunapee in his speed boat and put on a firework display especially for us! He was having this huge mansion built in the grounds of an old yacht club (using stone especially flown over from Belgium!), and there was even a mountain nearby that his family owned. In fact, the Tallaricos seemed to own the entire area!''

Welch also got a guided tour of Tyler's collection of guns and antique weapons, some of them having seen active service in Vietnam. He found the hyperactive extrovert a fascinating subject, although he did feel the scorn of the singer when he refused to indulge in the endless lines of cocaine Tyler snorted throughout the interview.

''I went from being a really interesting character, due to the fact that I knew The Yardbirds, into a boring old English fuddy-duddy after that!'' Welch chuckles.

Aerosmith eventually arrived in Britain on Saturday October 9, 1976, four days before the start of the tour. Tickets for the four shows – Liverpool Empire on October 13, followed by shows at Glasgow Apollo, Birmingham Odeon and London's Hammersmith Odeon, with homegrown act Phoenix (formed by guitarist John Verity from the ashes of Argent) in support – hadn't exactly gone like free beer in an Irish pub, and a last-gasp advertisement campaign was thrown into motion by David Krebs in order to fill any vacant seats.

'Hey Britain, wake up! This is America's greatest rock 'n' roll band!' screamed the slogan, and while Krebs later shuddered at the thought of such a crass hype line, he was nonetheless determined to land a metaphorical punch to the gut of Britain's so-far apathetic media and public.

''If Steven Tyler looked like Steven Tyler and not Mick Jagger,'' Krebs complained to *Sounds*, ''this band would be twice as big here as they are now. Ted Nugent didn't have to fight the natural desire of the British to say to an American band, 'Hey look, you're a rip-off'.''

The advertising slogan, he admitted . . . ''was a bullshit line. But I couldn't afford a half-full house at the Hammersmith Odeon even less than I could afford having Aerosmith's head chopped off in this media-conscious country.''

Aerosmith's head, however, was put on the block of press contempt as the UK tour unfolded. Those who attended the shows now consider the memory with affection, but reviews weren't universally favourable at all, as Lemmy remembers only too well.

''I went to the Hammersmith show and actually thought they were quite good,'' he laughs. ''But they were slagged unmercifully by the papers. One guy said Tyler looked like 'an au pair girl doing the hoovering', because he used to wear a leotard with a bustle on the backside and he used to push his mike-stand around the stage. It was cruel, but very funny . . .''

After the Hammersmith show Tyler threw a tantrum, smashing up his dressing room after a huge row with his girlfriend of the moment, *Playboy* centrefold Bebe Buell, the noted 'close companion' of many a rock star before him.

''The best bit was,'' Doug Smith smiles, ''seeing Tyler suddenly get embarrassed at what he'd done, and getting down on his knees with Bebe to clear all the food up that he'd thrown all over the place!''

The tantrum may have been a flash of frustration, it could have been a drug-induced explosion or it may have simply been a well-

A beginner's guide to America's hottest band. By GEOFF BARTON

UPFRONT ON AEROSMITH

rehearsed rock 'n' roll cliché, but whatever it was it highlighted the bizarre behaviour of Steven Tyler which increasingly tested the patience of those who came into contact with him.

"He wasn't the easiest person to work with because he always demanded 110 per cent," says Bob 'Nitebob' Czaykowski, the band's sound engineer throughout the mid-seventies, "but he was difficult in an interesting way because he always wanted to know everything. Soundchecks were intense battles . . . and he even had a pair of headphones behind the drum riser which were connected directly to me on the mixing desk out front, so he could call me during the show and ask questions about the sound.

"I remember the Birmingham Odeon show – the audience just stood there, shouting sarcastic comments like 'TURN IT UP!', because it was so loud. So in the middle of the show Steven called me up shouting 'Make it louder!' I tried to reason with him, telling him the crowd was just being sarcastic because it was too loud already, but he didn't understand and got real mad. Sometimes we'd have real shouting matches during the middle of a show!"

Others who encountered Steven Tyler for the first time weren't particularly enamoured of him at all.

"He just wasn't a very nice person," says Richard Ogden, "although at the time I didn't know that his mood swings and bad attitude problem was the result of his addiction to hard drugs. The band weren't all like that; Tom Hamilton was an extremely nice guy, a real gentleman, and Brad and Joey were OK too. But Tyler and Joe Perry were very much into the 'big star' trip, and I'd never experienced anything like that before. I mean, Ted Nugent was the antithesis of that attitude – very helpful, very friendly – but Aerosmith were hell to work with. They immediately put everyone's back up, and I must say that out of all the bands that Heavy Publicity handled, Aerosmith were my least favourite.

"It was also incredibly difficult to get the press to take them seriously, too," he continues, "because of the whole 'Stones rip-off' thing. And because they were huge in America they didn't realise the importance of working to get the press on their side; they didn't see it was essential to have two of three front covers in order to raise their profile, and a lot of the time they refused to do interviews. So not only did they alienate the press, they alienated their PR company as well."

The band did fare a little better on the Continent though, a whirlwind visit taking them to Cologne Sartory Saele on October 20 followed by Erlangen

Stadthalle, Stockholm Concert Hall, Amsterdam New Rai, Offenbach Stadthalle, Ludwigshafen Friedrich Ebert Hall, Zurich Volkshaus and Paris Pavilion Theatre on November 1. But when they finally left for the sanctuary of the States it was with more of a scuttle than a strut.

"They lost a fortune on that tour," says Doug Smith. "I mean, the private plane that they flew around in (a 45-seater Airbus hired from Southend, the kind usually used to carry football teams) was costing them £18,000 a night, and all they were making from the shows was a paltry two or three thousand here and there. In the States they could earn 10 times that per night – literally! – and even more from the huge stadium festivals that they were doing quite regularly.

"Not surprisingly, the band weren't too keen to hurry back to Europe. Krebs couldn't see the logic

of working over here because he viewed it as a fragmented territory of tiny nations and not as one big continent which, if broken, could be almost as lucrative as the United States. The whole thing seemed to him like a waste of time and money."

Back home, however, the wounds of an unsuccessful foreign venture were about to be healed by the success of another single. 'Walk This Way', the rapping rave-up from 'Toys In The Attic', was re-released during November and reached number 10 on the US charts just around the turn of the year. It was just the kind of confirmation the band needed to convince them of immortality, and they celebrated by sinking deeper into their toxic trenches, exhausted after nearly five years on the road non-stop and burnt out by all the money-no-object excesses of rock superstardom. Aerosmith, it seemed, were doing F.I.N.E.

Above: Dinner with the Queen . . . Aerosmith dine out with members of the 'new' English rock group.

CHAPTER FIVE

DOING F.I.N.E

ITH ONE EYE ON THEIR fatigue and another on their burgeoning drug problems, Aerosmith's management decided to whisk their boys away from the touring treadmill for a while and give them a well-deserved breather for the greater part of 1977. But first there was a commitment in Japan to honour – the band's first visit to the Far East, and one which typically didn't quite go as planned.

"Aerosmith were so huge at this point that they got used to getting whatever they demanded," says 'Nitebob', who incidentally got his nickname working for The New York Dolls during their all-night rehearsal sessions, "and one of the things they always demanded on their 'rider' was turkey on the bone. They were tired of getting turkey that'd already been sliced, so it had to be ON THE BONE!

"OK, so in Japan turkey doesn't exist, right? Not only that but it's real difficult to import poultry into Japan. But the band had demanded turkey so the promoter, Mr Udo, went to a great deal of trouble to get some for them. Anyway, at the first show the guys checked out the turkey and found it wasn't on the bone, so they flipped out and wrecked the dressing room . . . which is unheard of in Japan! The Japanese were really offended by it, it was a major insult and they weren't invited back for years. Mr Udo still talks about that episode today!"

Despite initial worries that the rest of the tour would be pulled after the incident at Maebashi on January 29, Aerosmith managed to complete all of the outstanding dates, hitting Tokyo, Nagoya, Fukoaka, Kyoto, Osaka and then Tokyo's famous Budokan again on February 9, all the shows being opened by Japan's own Bow Wow (now known as Vow Wow). Then it was back home for a few domestic dates during the Spring, and then . . . finally . . . rest. The temptation was to sling them straight back into the studio to record another money-spinning album while their popularity was at its peak, but even David Krebs knew that to test the band's stamina further at this point would be to play Russian Roulette with their very existence.

Besides, Aerosmith wanted a break to be able to spend time counting the hundreds of acres their 'financial advisers' had acquired for them, to explore their huge mansion houses which they'd rarely visited, and to play with their ultra-expensive rock star toys – private planes,

innumerable sports cars and plush home recording studios.

Joe Perry's 16-track home studio even played host to ex-New York Doll David Johansen's return to recording after leaving the group in 1975, with Jack Douglas taking charge of the controls – an ironic about-turn in the fortunes of a man who was once the envy of his Boston rivals.

But after a few months at home the band began to get itchy feet again, anxious for the buzz that playing before push-over punters every night creates.

"Imagine being on the road for five years solid and then going home," said Tyler. "You roll over on your bed and dial room service. It's really nuts!"

"It's also nuts being home for a couple of months because you start feeling really restless," added Tom. "After a few days of sitting around I start wondering why nothing's happening. It's a conflict between dying to get off the road and not being able to live on it."

But before they could hit the road again Aerosmith had a recording commitment to oblige, and plans for their fifth album were revealed. Krebs had decided that rather than let the band loose in the centre of Manhattan at the Record Plant again, the seclusion and serenity of somewhere more remote might provide better working conditions for the band in their present erratic state. But the plan backfired badly . . .

Aerosmith installed themselves in an abandoned 300-room monastery called The Cenacle in Armonk, upstate New York, and thereafter spent months finding reasons not to work. Most of the time was spent waiting for Tyler to get himself together enough to write some lyrics, although by now the singer was in such a stupor he would lock himself in the monastery's tower, spending days shooting at animals in the grounds with a shotgun.

His chief recollection now of those wasted months is of "this huge bottle of tuinols which I hid under the sink," but such excesses almost caught up with him when one day he slumped over his gun in a drugged daze and very nearly shot himself.

The project hadn't exactly got off to a perfect start in the first place. Before he left for The Cenacle, Joe Perry had spent a week at home making a demo of six song ideas which he'd recorded on a cassette. By the time he got to the studio he not only couldn't find the cassette, but he couldn't remember how the songs went either.

"That's where my head was at," said Perry. "It was like, 'I've got my drugs right here, but where

the hell is the cassette?'''

His wife Elissa found the tape in a biscuit tin a little while later. ''God knows how it got there,'' Perry remarked.

''That whole period was just a crazy time,'' Tom Hamilton explained. ''We ended up like a bunch of kids, playing 'hide and seek' and stuff!''

The cost of hiring the studio for months on end, meanwhile, was soaring higher and higher, and frustration at the behaviour of Tyler and Perry in particular was beginning to sow the seeds of unrest within the band. With the benefit of hindsight, Hamilton reckons that whole muddled period was ''the beginning of our break-up.''

Nevertheless, the hulking Aerosmith machine was mobilised once again in the autumn of 1977 for a batch of festival dates in Europe – a venture which Krebs hoped would improve the band's international reputation and cost less than their trek the previous year.

''A fat chance,'' according to Doug Smith. ''They arrived like something straight out of *Spinal Tap* – their own aeroplane, a fleet of limos, an army of girlfriends and wives, an endless road crew, masses and masses of equipment . . . we had two tractor trailers just carrying their backline! Looking back on it now, it was hilarious!''

The first stop for the band was in Belgium where the venue for their first gig for some time was the Biltzen Festival, a mortifying mudbath of concentration camp proportions, complete with brutal barbed-wire cage corralling 12,000 pathetic, rain-drenched P.O.W.-type punters. Journalist Nick Kent, reviewing the third day of the event for the *NME*, suggested that the whole circus ''may

well end rightfully eulogised as the most systematically harrowing, tortuous excuse for a rock festival ever promoted in the Western hemisphere.'' And performances from the likes of Ted Nugent, Uriah Heep, the Ian Gillan Band, Colosseum and Graham Parker And The Rumour, it seemed, failed to lift the gloom from an audience knee-deep in the quagmire.

''Krebs was so worried about what Steven Tyler might do when he saw all the mud in the backstage area that he went out and bought everybody green wellies and green overcoats,'' Doug Smith recalls in between side-splitting wheezes, ''the bands, the Aerosmith crew, the Ted Nugent crew, everyone. We looked like an army on manoeuvres!''

The band, meanwhile, arrived at the site late after fog delayed their flight from Boston, and declined to mingle with almost anyone except their wives – Joey with April, Tom with Terry, Brad with Laurie and Steven, as striking as ever in a long tan coat and glittery Wellingtons, with girlfriend Bebe. Joe Perry, now officially recognised as 'the moody one', sat alone with his blonde spouse Elissa, keeping such a low profile that the *NME* scribe was moved to express concern for his well-being.

Whatever the odd, unsociable off-stage demeanour of the band, on-stage they managed to gel reasonably well despite the appalling conditions. A set culled mainly from 'Rocks' and 'Toys . . .' appeased the blighted Belgians, and a similar feat at the Lorelei Festival near Frankfurt in Germany also added to their reputation, although celebrations were muted after news arrived that Elvis Presley had died back home in America the same day, Tuesday August 16. As a mark of respect a minute's silence was called for between sets by co-headliners The Doobie Brothers and Aerosmith.

Back at the airport in Germany, Tyler was enjoying a skirmish with Customs officers after having his collar felt for possession of cannabis . . .

''The guy found my stash of hash,'' Tyler joked later, ''so I blew it all in front of him.''

Perry, however, got away scot-free. ''I always used to say I would never ask someone else to do what I wouldn't do myself, but we'd have so much stuff in our pockets that I'd get to the gate and give it to one of the roadies.''

Other drug-smuggling tricks included sewing them into the hems of T-shirts or placing them in specially-sewn folds in Steven's many scarves – a method used when the band finally made it to Blighty for the Reading Festival during August.

''You know that little scarf I used to wear on-stage?'' Tyler confessed to the British press recently. ''It was filled with tuinols. It was like a condom. It had a little hole at the top. I would hold onto them while we were playing. Feel them, count them . . .''

It was just as well then that the band made it through Customs at Heathrow. In London they busied themselves with a bit of sightseeing and shopping – Tyler flitting along to the Islington antique market, and then to Harrods where a

Aerosmith on stage at the Reading Festival, August 1977.

"I think they're the best rock 'n' roll band I've ever seen."

BOB CATLEY, MAGNUM

100-year-old cognac was among several goodies bagged. And then later at the band's hideout, Anouska Hempel's Blakes hotel in South Kensington, the singer told *Sounds* why Aerosmith had bothered to return to the country which had handed them such an unflinching critical flogging the last time they visited.

"You can be the biggest band in America, but if you don't try to break Britain you've got no guts," he explained, while Krebs ranted on about the fact that it was more fun trying to break Britain than selling out a second show in Cincinnati.

The bottom line was that Aerosmith wanted to be successful in Britain purely for the prestige, and if appearing at a lowly, ego-deflating position on the Reading bill was what it took, then that's how it was going to be. Besides, Tyler was quick to point out, "It gives you an edge . . . it'll be like when we used to open up for bands like Mott The Hoople. It'll bring the fun right back in . . ."

The fun of the festival, however, was severely dampened once again by heavy rain which inconvenienced Krebs and Doug Smith to the point where they had to take the drastic step of leaving their limo sinking in the mud to slip and slide across the sodden site on foot.

"It was horrendous," Smith winces, "although the band's spirits were slightly raised by the huge billboards CBS had managed to erect, advertising the event. We had to have a good promotional idea to match the 'boxing' one the year before, so I got these massive AEROSMITH 'ROCKS' AT READING banners made up. I couldn't get that many as they were so bloody expensive, but I got two of them put up on the route that I knew their limos were going to take from the hotel to the gig, and that freaked them out completely!"

Another gimmick designed to appeal to the band was the double-decker London bus which CBS had converted into a hospitality area for band and liggers alike. The band's crew, meanwhile, didn't offer much hospitality.

"We were all having a drink on the bus when suddenly everyone was ordered off it by some security guy," says Richard Ogden, who was managing The Motors at the time, as well as co-ordinating Aerosmith's PR. "The next thing I knew my wife and I were physically thrown down the stairs by a roadie and kicked off the bus – even though it was absolutely pissing down with rain!"

The same day Ogden was punched by a bouncer after trying to get into the 'guests' enclosure to see Aerosmith's set, despite brandishing proof that he actually worked for the band.

Indeed, by this stage Aerosmith had surrounded themselves with a battle-hardened, no-nonsense entourage who formed a fearsome protective

THIRTY THREE

shield around their employers. There was tour manager Bob 'Kelly' Kelleher, a smooth, 18-stone New Yorker and stage manager Joe Baptista, an elder statesman type and a former rigger from Barnum And Bailey's circus in America, who'd actually worked in Britain during the Second World War. And there was Henry Smith, at this time 'first lieutenant' to Kelleher as 'assistant tour director', who remembers the crew with lasting affection.

"There were more than a few characters there," he muses, "and when we hit countries like England it was very much like an army invading enemy territory. If anyone got in our way we usually steamrollered straight through them!"

Photographers at the event that year also felt the wrath of the crew's heavy-handed approach, being ordered out of the photo-pit in front of the stage so the band's wives could have somewhere to dance without getting dirty.

"It was hysterical," recalls infamous snap-chap Ross Halfin, then more of a whipper-snapper,

"watching all these birds balancing and dancing on these tiny planks of wood in their stack-heeled boots and satin dresses, while all around was a sea of mud. We were all killing ourselves!"

The band, meanwhile, had hit the stage to the strains of the *Psycho* theme and launched straight into 'Mama Kin', spitting like a fireball of raw energy before crashing into 'S.O.S. (Too Bad)' with barely a pause for breath. Next, with Tyler wrapping his inflatable lips around a harmonica, 'Big Ten Inch Record' swung its jazzy groove across the wet Reading masses and romped into a head-on collision with 'Lord Of The Thighs'. And then after a brief pause, Joey Kramer conjured up a drum riff that led into a no-frills run-through of 'Lick And A Promise'.

Not surprisingly, an albeit sluggish and dangerously out-of-tune version of 'Dream On' drew some cheers of recognition from the rather subdued crowd, and then 'Walkin' The Dog' and 'Sweet Emotion' paved the way for 'Walk This Way' to receive possibly the biggest roar of the set.

Then came a surprise: "Y'all getcha tape recorders goin' – we're gonna do somethin' from

our new album,'' Tyler teased, and 'Draw The Line' made its début on a British stage, sounding fresh and frisky. 'Same Old Song And Dance' followed, then 'Train Kept A Rollin'' with Tyler getting the audience to chant the 'all night long' section and Perry slotting in a quick burst of the 'Combination' finale.

Lastly, the band obliged prolonged calls for an encore with a blistering 'Toys In The Attic', finally trooping off stage with the majority of the crowd firmly on their side.

The critics, however, weren't convinced and dished out a mass slagging which had the *NME* wondering if the band would ''even bother to demean themselves by touring here yet again.'' And so it was with a bitter taste in their mouths that Aerosmith headed home to prepare for the release of 'Draw The Line', safe in the knowledge that their management wouldn't risk the hassle of another trip to Europe again.

* * *

In America though, Aerosmith's popularity was hitting new heights. 'Draw The Line' was released in the US just before Christmas and went platinum faster than any 'Smith release to date, the wave of public support for the band blindly washing over the fact that the record was far from a worthy follow-up to 'Rocks', coming on rather like the hangover after a party. In spite of having the best part of a year and over a million dollars spent on its recording, the album sounded sloppy and lacklustre, a nasty-but-true reflection of the state of the band.

The package opened promisingly enough – 'Draw The Line' and 'I Wanna Know Why' (both prime Tyler/Perry cuts) scything into the memory as semi-classics, the latter especially kicking into the kind of casual, good-time groove that Aerosmith had copyrighted from The Stones by now.

But the rather messy, stumbling boogie of 'Critical Mass' – a Tyler/Hamilton/Jack Douglas collaboration that never quite held together – let the side down, and 'Get It Up' (with L.A. Jets singer Karen Lawrence on backing vocals) jerked uneasily on a riff that didn't quite seem to fit into the song. Joe Perry, it appeared, wasn't far behind Tyler in the 'out to lunch' stakes, and the inclusion of his simple, repetitive rocker 'Bright Light Fright' – with Perry himself singing lead vocals – was indicative of his personal lack of quality control.

'It's the dawn of the day and I'm crashed and I'm smashed/As it is I'm feeling like my chips are cashed/All of my clothes are strewn all over the room/The crisis at hand is I'm all out of zoom', went the words to 'Bright Light Fright', and as the song itself was one of the poorest excuses for an Aerosmith track ever recorded, you can quite easily believe them.

Side two wasn't much better. 'Kings And Queens' was the standout song, a sprawling, spooky epic pieced together by Hamilton, Kramer, Whitford, Tyler and Douglas, and utilising the different textures of piano (Tyler), mandolin (Douglas) and banjo (Paul Prestopino) particularly well beneath the usual rock-hard back-beat. And

'Sight For Sore Eyes', an idea attributed equally to Tyler, Perry and Douglas with David Johansen, possessed some of the funky charm that fuelled 'Walk This Way' and 'Last Child'.

But 'The Hand That Feeds' featured a horribly overstretched Tyler vocal, and the band's interpretation of 'Milk Cow Blues', the 1934 Kokomo Arnold song which Elvis Presley made famous in the sixties, was as pointless as a busted pencil.

Later, Perry admitted that 'Draw The Line' represented a low point in the band's recording career.

''From the inside I didn't think anything was wrong,'' he confessed, ''but from the outside you could see everything; you can hear the music get cloudy. Listen to 'Draw The Line' – the focus of 'Rocks' is completely gone. If I kept a journal I couldn't have done a better job of showing exactly when we started going south. It wasn't funny.''

The humour of the front cover design – grotesque, comical caricatures of the Famous Five drawn by cartoonist Al Hirschfeld – didn't go to waste though, and to complete the marketing muscle this time around a new Aerosmith logo was stamped onto all merchandise.

''When I saw the 'Get Your Wings' logo I went 'What is this shit?','' says Ray Tabano. ''The idea was good but the actual result was terrible. So I thought up a way of changing it around to make it look cool; I used the Harley Davidson wings, added the little star in the middle and there it was, the official Aerosmith logo which you still see today.''

In the UK the album was to be released on January 10, beginning a busy period for Leber-Krebs, who also had Rex releasing their 'Where Do We Go From Here' LP the same month and Ted Nugent spitting out his 'Live Gonzo' package on February 10. The music press ad for 'Draw The Line' pleaded with the British fans to shelve their prejudices and give the band a chance . . .

'''Draw The Line' invites you to experience at first hand the music with which America has challenged British rock dominance,'' it ran. ''You can draw the line at the established British names, but in doing so you'll be ignoring some of the best American hard rock you're ever likely to hear . . .''

It was stern stuff, but it still failed to bowl the Brits over. Nevertheless, with cash registers ringing to the tune of 'Draw The Line' all over the States, Aerosmith prepared to clean up the US market once and for all in 1978 by headlining the second California Jam concert at the Ontario Speedway track on March 18. Four years earlier the event had been launched with a bill that featured Deep Purple, ELP, The Eagles, Black Oak Arkansas, Black Sabbath and The Chamber Brothers, and crowd estimates of 250,000 made it one of the biggest rock festivals ever. Now it was the turn of Aerosmith, Santana, Heart, Dave Mason, Ted Nugent, Mahogany Rush and

Rubicon (the forerunner of Night Ranger, featuring Brad Gillis and Jack Blades), this time in front of an estimated 350,000 punters.

It should have been the highlight of Aerosmith's career to that date. Instead it wasn't far from being a shambles, as footage of the show available on video – *Video Scrapbook* – reveals. Tyler later recalled The Jam – the year's biggest and most prestigious rock event – as . . . "a blackout. I remember arriving in a helicopter, I was kind of drifting in and out, coming in at 100 feet up and I couldn't see the edges of the crowd. All I knew was that I was in the air, I couldn't make out why . . ."

And that confused recollection came as no great shock to journalist Sylvie Simmons, who interviewed Tyler and Hamilton backstage before the show (Perry wouldn't be in the same room as the singer), and found Tyler snorting up mammoth mounds of cocaine off a full-page photo of his own face in a Japanese magazine! Needless to say, the record company representative who was supposed to be supervising the interview had to be given mouth-to-mouth resuscitation . . .

Having completed the biggest show of their lives, Aerosmith took some time off to appear in Robert Stigwood's dreadful film based on The Beatles' 'Sgt. Pepper's Lonely Hearts Club Band'. As an attempted late seventies answer to *Tommy*, the film starred two of the biggest names of the day, The Bee Gees and Peter Frampton as the goodies, with Alice Cooper and Aerosmith type-cast as the baddies, the 'Smiths portraying the notorious Future Villain Band.

"We shot it in Hollywood in about a week," Henry Smith recalls, "and it was great fun. Steven did all his own stunts – like falling off a 20-foot tower on to an airbed – but I remember there was a bit of a disagreement as to how the movie would end . . ."

The screenplay dictated that Tyler would be killed off in a fight with Peter Frampton, but after insisting that "Nobody ever beats Aerosmith!", the plot was altered to smooth over an ego or two.

"We went through that part of the movie carefully," explained Tom Hamilton, "and had them change it so that it didn't come off too much like Frampton directly overcoming Steven physically. He just lost his balance and fell . . ."

"And the outcome," Henry Smith adds, "was left vague enough to allow Steven to escape the film with his superstar reputation intact!"

Meanwhile, one of the main reasons for Aerosmith's involvement in the film had come to fruition in New York. The band had the chance to record The Beatles' 'Come Together' for the film soundtrack with The Fab Four's original producer, George Martin, and relished the opportunity like born-again teenagers. On an otherwise appallingly lacklustre album Aerosmith's track, as well as Earth Wind And Fire's reading of 'Got To Get You Into My Life', were the standout items.

"It was a great thrill for them to be actually working with the guy who produced some of their all-time favourite records," says Henry Smith, "and they had a ball."

"We'd already done a couple of Beatles songs in our repertoire," said Tyler, "so it was really easy for us to get up there and do a song like 'Come Together'. We didn't listen to The Beatles' album beforehand, we just did it from how we remembered it in the past. We just sat down, got drunk, and did it in six takes."

The song was released as a single and stayed on the American charts for three months, while the

Below, left: Hamilton, Tyler and Perry at the *Sergeant Pepper* launch in Los Angeles, 1978. Right: Aerosmith perform for a few of their intimate friends at the height of their popularity. Below: George Martin, producer of Aerosmith's version of 'Come Together.'

"Aerosmith? Yeeeeaah! I love 'em!"

JON BON JOVI

band hit the road again during May for a proposed back-to-the-people tour of the clubs and small theatres. It was their intention to prove to their fans that Aerosmith hadn't lost touch with reality in their current state of megastardom.

The band had first become disillusioned with huge stadium shows during that Pontiac Stadium gig in 1976. ''Honest to God,'' said Tyler, ''you could have flown an aeroplane into that stadium. While the other band were playing Joe and I went for a walk around the place, because Joe had just bought a new movie camera and I wanted to see how it looked to the kids. Well, we got halfway around and the stage . . . well, the only way I could tell it was a stage was because there was this little bit lit up! It was awful and it really pissed us off.''

So under the pseudonym Dr Jones And The Interns, Aerosmith played a date at The Starwood Club in Los Angeles (later described by Joe Perry as ''one of the best gigs we ever did'') and another at The Paradise Club in Boston on August 9, but the original idea of doing a whole tour was soon blown out, and the venture ground to a halt with tension in the band beginning to force a few cracks.

Nevertheless Aerosmith had a genuine high regard for their fans, and the story of the band's own attorney going to a jail in Fort Wayne to bail out and pay the fines of 50 kids who were arrested at an Aerosmith concert for smoking dope verifies their concern. Aerosmith tackled the problem of wanting to cut down on touring while allowing as many fans as possible to see them by deciding to embark on a series of big stadium dates after all, but this time every effort was made to ensure the crowd got the best deal possible, and they installed huge projection screens and extra speakers around the stadium to allow even those at the very back to hear and see properly.

By the middle of the summer, with both the 'California Jam II' album (featuring 'Same Old Song And Dance', 'Draw The Line' and 'Chip

Away The Stone') and the 'Sgt. Pepper . . .' soundtrack hitting the record stores, Aerosmith appeared at another of the rock festival packages which had become the fashion in North America during the late seventies. On the weekend of July 4 – American Independence Day – they headlined the original Texas World Music Festival (nicknamed the Texxas Jam) at the Cotton Bowl in Dallas, joining forces with stablemates Ted Nugent and Mahogany Rush, The Atlanta Rhythm Section, Heart, Head East, Journey, Eddie Money and Van Halen to provide 15 hours of music to over 150,000 fans during the two days.

Once again though, Aerosmith's set was well below par – the show eventually came out on video (Live Texxas Jam '78) for all to see – and they were clearly in a sorry physical and mental state. Tyler, dressed appropriately in sombre black instead of the usual flamboyant stripes, lumbered around the stage like a lost drunk, failing to remember most of the words let alone hit the right notes. His microphone, previously used as a cross between a phallic symbol and a majorette's baton, was now merely a crutch to lean on (although Joey Kramer's bass drum found itself keeping the singer upright during 'Same Old Song And Dance'), and so oblivious was he to the general proceedings that he hardly noticed guest guitarist Ted Nugent stealing Brad Whitford's solo in 'Milk Cow Blues'.

The 'Draw The Line' tour – on which the band was supplemented by keyboard kid Mark Radice –

Kramer's drum solo was boring! Egos had certainly been blown out of all proportion, to the point where Perry and Tyler would refuse to even sit in the same limo together. In the midst of the madness the rift between the permanently peeved pair was escalating into all-out war.

''We used to fight on-stage,'' Tyler admitted. ''Joe could torment me to death by not giving me a line of dope. So then I'd wait and go over and push him around while he was playing, and he would hit me with his guitar. He stuck the end of a guitar string through my lower lip once, so I spat blood all over him . . .''

''It got pretty silly,'' Henry Smith sighs. ''Plus by this time the wives were really getting in the way of everything. Steven was married to Cyrinda Fox by now – she was the ex-wife of David Johansen, a.k.a. Buster Poindexter – and Joe still had Elissa with him, and the two of them just didn't get along. I'd even have to get to know their menstrual cycles, so I knew when to keep the ones with PMT away from the others. It was a very delicate operation because there would be personality clashes between all the wives at different points, and that of course would get the guys at each other's throats. It ended up with everyone travelling in separate limos, and hardly speaking to each other in between shows. You needed an Honours Degree in diplomacy to tour manage Aerosmith in those days!''

A degree in chemistry wouldn't have gone to waste either, as the band's huge personal stashes of 'substances' became part of the furniture in the Aerosmith camp. As a result there were plenty of near-death experiences to contend with too, Tyler and Perry almost racing each other to some kind of suicidal goal.

One time Perry had a hit of drugs just as his private plane was cleared to go down the runway; he suddenly suffered a huge convulsion and the flight had to be aborted, with Perry being carried away by the police. Another time Tyler went driving through a wood with a loaded shotgun in his jeep, had a seizure, snapped his foot down on the gas and crashed into a tree. To balance things up there was the occasion Perry injected himself with codeine, waking up in a doorway hours later with the needle still sticking out of his arm. And then there's the story about Tyler falling off stage, breaking his ankle, and being so out of it he got up and didn't feel a thing.

''Now you know why they were called 'The Toxic Twins','' says Henry Smith. ''They'd do whatever drugs were in front of them. For Steven one gramme of cocaine was too much, but 100 grammes wasn't enough. Sometimes I'd find him slumped in his dressing room just before a gig and I would have the job of trying to bring him round. I'd hold two fingers before his eyes and he'd swear there were four. I'd have the promoter in the dressing room shouting, 'There has GOT to be a show tonight or else . . .!', and I'd go 'It's OK, he'll be fine', all the while thinking 'Oh God, how the hell am I going to get out of this one?!'

''Sometimes, I'd literally have to carry Steven to the stage. But he was worried about his fans

continued throughout the latter half of 1978, with bands like Anglo-Aussie upstarts AC/DC in support. But rumblings of dissatisfaction and dissension within the ranks soon grew to volcanic proportions.

''The whole Aerosmith machine was a monster,'' says Henry Smith. ''The sheer size of the entourage and equipment meant it wasn't really possible to travel around the country any more. By this time we had our own Lear jet, so we'd base ourselves at, say, the Whitehall Hotel in Chicago, and fly to each gig and back every night. That was easier because it was getting harder and harder to get all the guys and their wives up every morning, plus the amount of gear the guys wanted to carry with them was ridiculous; they'd have stereo systems that'd be, like, five feet long and two feet high in flight cases!''

Other excesses had also come to light, with Geoff Barton claiming in *Sounds* that . . . ''This band are the worst example of the superstar syndrome I've ever come across . . . After all, this is the band I once saw at Toronto's CNE stadium travel the 100 yards from the backstage dressing room caravans to the staircase leading up to the specially constructed stage in two limos!''

Barton, incidentally, was banned from the after-show party that night for saying that Joey

seeing him in that state, so I'd pretend to be giving him a 'piggyback', doing it just for fun. The truth of it was he couldn't walk, but then once he was on-stage he'd go into 'automatic' and put on a great show.''

It didn't always happen like that though. Often Tyler would simply keel over mid-set, and Brad Whitford retains the painful memory of one such occasion.

''I saw Steven drop like a stone, he was out cold, and my heart and stomach just sank. It was just an awful moment, because you really get scared for someone . . .''

Joey Kramer also winces when he remembers the time Tyler turned the band into a laughing stock during a gig at the Anaheim Stadium near Disneyland in southern California.

''I don't know what Steven had been doing all day, but as always he was on something. We were about four songs into the show and he stopped everyone from playing. He went over and sat on the front of the stage with his legs dangling down and started telling a joke to the audience. I tried to start another song, and he'd tell me to stop. Then he'd go back and talk to the audience.''

It had all gone too far, although in commercial terms at least Aerosmith were still one of the hottest bands in America. Their 'Live Bootleg' album became their sixth platinum record shortly after its release in November 1978, proving that the loyalty of their fans was strong enough to override the quality of their product.

Having said that though, the shoddy, thrown-together package of live recordings which constituted the 'Live Bootleg' was more the result of an attempt to beat the bootleggers at their own game than of careless, haphazard compiling. The material was raw, raucous and rougher than a sandpaper G-string, and included several rarities: a cover of James Brown's 'Mother Popcorn' recorded in April 1973 at Boston's Paul's Mall (which Tyler credits as being ''The first club we played''); a rehearsal of 'Come Together' at the Wherehouse hideout in August 1978; a version of band-friend Richie Supa's 'Chip Away The Stone' which Aerosmith included in their set through 1978; and various other recordings from around 1977 and 1978.

''I was getting ticked off at seeing lots of bootlegs,'' Tyler explained. ''Some of them had great covers but no attitude, which was what we were all about. It was time to jump on it, so I had some rubber stamps made, we went up to the CBS art room and stamped the logo on a piece of paper, and that was our sleeve designed!''

The record pleaded for legitimacy, but cynics might have argued that the whole 'Live Bootleg' idea was specifically engineered to allow the band enough breathing space/sobering up time before another studio album was recorded. Once again there was a question mark over whether Tyler and Perry could patch up their differences for long enough to record another album, and as 1979 loomed those who'd predicted some kind of Aerosmith Armageddon were starting to place their bets . . .

CHAPTER SIX

A PERMANENT VACATION?

EROSMITH BEGAN 1979 THE only way they knew how – treading the boards with gruelling regularity. However, with internal relations worsening all the time and the behaviour of certain members getting more and more bizarre, the touring pace was slowed in an attempt to avoid complete combustion.

The band eventually began work on their sixth studio album, 'Night In The Ruts', during the spring, using the Wherehouse for pre-production before going into Mediasound Studios on Manhattan's West 57th Street to begin the recording proper. English producer Gary Lyons, who'd previously worked with Foreigner, Humble Pie and Lone Star, was chosen by Krebs and CBS. He had a six-album production deal with the label and seemed the ideal man for the production and engineering job, the thinking being that having one man do the two jobs would lessen the hassle in an already confused situation. The principal concern of everyone was that Aerosmith could be kept together for long enough to finish the record.

''It was a very strenuous process,'' Lyons reflects, ''because individually and collectively they all had their problems. Fame is sometimes harder to deal with than failure, and the guys were trying to get to grips with all that around this time. Although having all the wives and girlfriends getting in the way didn't help the situation at all.

''Of all of them, Tom Hamilton was the most stable, and Joey Kramer was OK too, but Steven and Joe Perry were at loggerheads, and so when Joe was in the studio Steven wouldn't show up, and vice versa. It was a very complicated set-up.

''Joe came in first and got all his guitar parts done and out of the way pretty early on. But I remember one night when he was trying to put the rhythm part to 'Chiquita' down his guitar kept going out of tune. So I kept stopping the tape, he'd re-tune his guitar and we'd be off again. Then it'd go out again, so he'd change his strings, put some carbon out of a pencil onto the nuts to stop them slipping, and start again. But it kept going out of tune for about four or five hours, until he got so frustrated and angry he threw it across the control room. When he'd calmed down enough he went

Top right: Perry's first solo album cover.

over and picked it up, and it was fine – it didn't go out of tune again for the rest of the session!''

But although Perry was ploughing on with his parts, the main problem was getting Tyler coherent enough to sing and write lyrics, and the massive amount of studio time the record company had block-booked for them was once again petering out unproductively. For Lyons it worked out well, because he was also working on the Grateful Dead's 'Go To Heaven' album at the same time in San Francisco, commuting back and forth from the East and West Coasts whenever it was most convenient, allowing Tyler a week or two here and there to try and get lyrics and melodies together. But finally, things got so expensive that the management saw no alternative to sending the band back out on the road again, to try and make back some of the money they'd wasted. It proved to be the straw that broke Joe Perry's back.

At a financial meeting just prior to the tour the management handed Perry a room service bill for an astonishing $80,000. They told him he was in debt to the band to the tune of $100,000, although if he did a solo album the advance would wipe his slate clean.

''I said, 'Fine, I'll make a solo album.' It was so dumb. I didn't need to make a solo album . . .''

It was inevitable that in his drugged-out state Tyler would see Perry's brazen stance of independence as an offensive gesture towards the band, and the fighting intensified accordingly.

''We never talked,'' said Tyler. ''I sat moaning to my old lady about him doing a solo record when I should have confronted him and maybe done a track on it. We were right in the middle of recording 'Night In The Ruts', paying to live in hotels when we had mansions just around the corner. We were all just totally shot.''

Everything came to an ugly head shortly after at a show in Cleveland, Ohio. The tension had been building towards a major showdown and backstage after the set the whole situation exploded.

''We had a band meeting,'' Tom Hamilton ponders, ''although it was not the best time and place for one, as we were all so red-faced and hyped-up after coming off stage . . .''

Plus, as Tyler remembers . . . ''We were so smacked out and drunk we played like shit on-stage. I was totally lost at the time. I couldn't write lyrics any more and I was cancelling gigs because I was doing too much opium, and when you do opium you can't sing because it screws up your voice box. All the pressures of the last 10 years, all the violence came out like a pressure hole exploding.''

An argument started, the wives pitched in, Joe's wife Elissa poured milk over Terry Hamilton, and all hell broke loose. Perry decided he'd sling his hook there and then.

''The drugs won,'' Tyler reflected. ''We split up over a glass of spilt milk – can you believe it?''

* * *

Stung by Tyler's criticism and urged along by the need to repay his debts, Joe Perry wasted no time in putting together a new band – The Joe Perry Project. He'd actually been working with a group of musicians on the side during the stuttering 'Night In The Ruts' saga, but now they became his full-time backing band: vocalist Ralph Mormon (who'd approached Perry at an Aerosmith gig hoping for hints about getting some work), bassist David Hull (an ex-Dirty Angel who Perry had known since the Boston bar days), and drummer Ronnie Stewart (another unknown who'd been working in a drum store for eight years).

With a hatful of ideas already down on tape (some of which were meant for 'Night In The Ruts'), Perry scampered swiftly into the studio with old friend Jack Douglas as co-producer, emerging later with 'Let The Music Do The Talking', his first solo album.

The record was in fact a fine statement of intent, sometimes fast and furious ('Life At A Glance'), sometimes slow and doomy ('The Mist Is Rising'), sometimes funky ('Rockin' Train'), sometimes purely a vehicle for Perry's whiplash guitar ('Break Song'). There was also, inevitably, a strong Aerosmith vein running through the tracks, and while 'Shooting Star' could quite easily have been a bona fide Aero-song, 'Ready On The Firing Line' actually featured a snippet of a riff which would appear on 'Night In The Ruts' during 'Chiquita'.

The album was released on Columbia Records in the States in March 1980, and The Project immediately took to the road to promote it. The live set usually began with 'Same Old Song And Dance', followed by 'Get The Lead Out' and a version of The New York Dolls' 'Pills', with 'Reefer Headed Woman', 'Bone To Bone' (both from 'Night In The Ruts'), 'Bright Light Fright' and 'Walk This Way' also cropping up throughout the show. Elsewhere, covers of Elvis Presley's 'Heartbreak Hotel' and The Stones'/Bobby Womack's 'All Over Now' usually found their way into the set, and of course there was also a fair proportion of 'Let The Music . . .' to be aired.

After one gig at the 3,000-seater Santa Monica Civic in California, Perry took time to reflect on his decision to leave Aerosmith.

''I had written the basic tracks for 'Night In The Ruts','' he told Sylvie Simmons, ''and they were cut with as much lead as I could put in without the

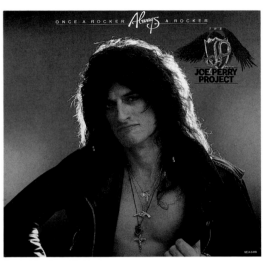

Top: The Joe Perry
project.
Right: Michael
Schenker – Perry's
replacement?

Tyler had in fact sent a telegram to Perry congratulating him on his new album, but there was no chance of the pair getting back together.

''I don't feel any link with the band at all,'' said Perry, although he did defend his decision to include so many 'Smith songs in his solo set. ''Those are my songs, I wrote the music. Those are some of my favourite riffs, and Ralph sings them better. I get off on it because this band plays them better than I have heard those songs played in a long while.''

Flushed with the freshness of his new Project, Perry eventually recorded two more solo albums. The first, 'I've Got The Rock 'n' Rolls Again' (recorded at the Boston Opera House with producer Bruce Botnick, and originally titled 'Soldier Of Fortune'), found new rhythm guitarist Charlie Farren handling lead vocals in place of Ralph Mormon (who'd been sacked, incidentally, by chronic alcoholic Perry for having a drink problem! The Project also briefly entertained ex-Revolver vocalist Joey Mala before Farren's arrival). And despite everything, it wasn't a bad effort, surfacing in June 1981 on Columbia and refining the sound of 'Let The Music . . .' even further with a metallic mixture of blues, boogie and ballsy R&B.

The third JPP album, 'Once A Rocker Always A Rocker', came out in September 1983 on the MCA label, and featured yet another line-up – vocalist Mach Bell, bassist Danny Hargrove and drummer Joe Pet. Self-produced and recorded at Blue Jay studios in Carlisle, Massachusetts, it was a touch more 'glam' than its predecessors (it even included a version of Marc Bolan's 'Bang A Gong'), and as such was the weakest of the three. It seemed as though it was time for yet another change in the life of Joe Perry . . .

* * *

Meanwhile back in the post-Perry Aerosmith camp, the band put the finishing touches to 'Night In The Ruts' as best they could. Tyler's old friend Richie Supa patched up some guitar bits, guitar technician Neil Thompson even chipped in with some six-string work, and at one point even ex-UFO guitarist Michael Schenker was considered as a replacement for Perry by Krebs and his new assistant Peter Mensch (who has since gone on to manage Def Leppard, Metallica and Dan Reed Network). Gary Lyons remembers it only too well . . .

''So one day Michael Schenker walks into the studio, dressed in black leather jacket, black leather trousers, black leather boots, blond hair, blue eyes . . . and just for a laugh I stopped the tape and said to him, 'Who do you think you are, goose-stepping in here wearing your Nazi uniform? Who won the war anyway? Go on – get outta here!' It was like that *Fawlty Towers* episode, right? But Schenker didn't find it funny, so he walked out.

''Minutes later, Peter Mensch came in and said Michael was upset, and asked me if I would apologise to him. I said, 'Sure', so he came back into the control room and I said, 'I'm sorry about

others. It was just taking Aerosmith so long to get that album out, and I was so fed up with that because in the meantime all during the summer we played these gigs and we couldn't play any of the new material because it wasn't ready. Instead we had to go back and do the same old songs.

''And then we had to cancel a European tour – we were supposed to come to England and do Knebworth with Led Zeppelin – because we had no album. And then we had to blow out an American tour . . . and *still* the album wasn't out!

''While all this had been going on I had been working with these other guys on this solo album, and there was resentment there from Aerosmith. They'd say, 'Why don't you go down and help Steven with that?' and I'd say 'I already did my part, I already wrote the tunes, what more do you want from me?'

''So it came down to me calling up Tom Hamilton and saying, 'It's off, I just don't think I'm going to be able to go on the road with you this time, I'm going to stick with my solo thing. I can't put up with it any more.' That was the last official

"They're just something else. Real good, down-to-earth, honest, bluesy rock 'n' roll. They're the business."

GARY JAMES, THUNDER

that, I was only joking . . . actually no, I wasn't joking, go on – piss off!' He stormed out of the studio again and refused to audition for the band after that!''

Somehow Lyons and the band did manage to finish the job off as professionally as they could under the circumstances. ''The atmosphere was weird,'' says Lyons, ''but I'd do little things to break the ice. I'd buy porno mags and cut out all the pictures to stick around the place. After about two weeks every tiny space was covered – the walls, the ceiling, the equipment, everything. And then as a joke someone bought me a double-ended dildo, about three foot long, which I put in pride of place on the mixing desk. It was OK until one day my assistant engineer, Peter Thea who was about

18 at the time, had his mum show up to take him out for lunch, and she nearly died of shock when she walked into the control room and saw this filth everywhere!''

Some humour also managed to filter through the most demanding of sessions too, and Lyons particularly remembers the final mix of 'Mia' . . .

''We'd worked all through the night because we knew that we had to be out of the studio by noon the next day, as someone else was coming in to do a session. So we were frantically putting the finishing touches to the track when we heard footsteps and voices on the tape, and we couldn't find out where the hell they were coming from, even though we checked each track on the multi-track machine and everything.

''As it turned out, the New York Telephone Company were doing some repairs on the studio's phone system, and the box where all the lines came in was in the same room where the echo plates were. So the echo plates were picking up these guys stomping around, and it was showing up in the control room!

''So then the guy who ran the studio came in and told us our time was up. But during all this, one of the band's roadies called George Schak had been amusing himself by sharpening the Q-tips which were used to clean tape-heads into darts, and blowing them through empty biro pens, like blow darts. When this guy came in ranting about us leaving, George blew this dart at him and it missed his face by about two inches, sticking in the wall behind him! This guy's face went white, and he was very nice to us after that – he let us stay as long as we wanted!''

By November 1979 'Night In The Ruts' was finally ready for release. Not surprisingly the album wasn't one of Aerosmith's best, yet considering the background of turmoil from whence it came, it wasn't that bad a record either. 'No Surprise', the opening track, was another minor Tyler/Perry classic, telling the story of how the band had found fame the hard way ('1971, we all heard the starter's gun/New York was such a pity but at Max's Kansas City we won'), and 'Chiquita' which followed also blazed a brilliant, brassy trail of glory on a riff which remains one of Perry's best.

Other Tyler/Perry contributions which worked well despite the lack of communication between the two were 'Cheese Cake', 'Three Mile Smile' and 'Bone To Bone (Coney Island White Fish Boy)'. But a cover of The Shangri-Las' 'Remember

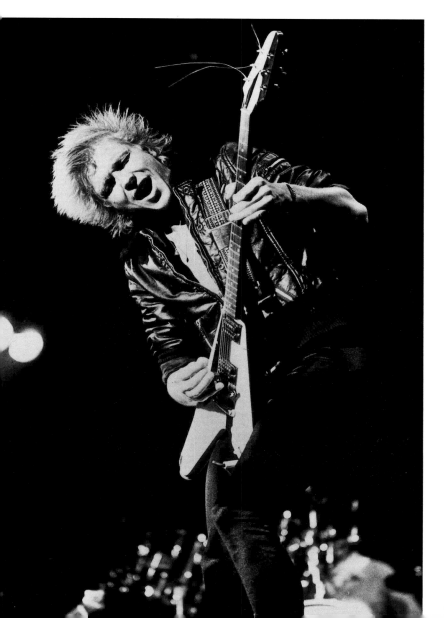

FORTY THREE

(Walking In The Sand)' sounded well out of place (even though one of the original Shangri-Las helped Tyler with the lyrics and melody), and the simple bluesy workout of 'Reefer Head Woman' (credited as 'Unknown' on the label, but actually written in 1945 by Lester Melrose, Joe Bennett and Willie Gillum) would've been better off kept for a B-side, indicating as it did just how thin on the ground top-notch original material actually was at the time.

To complete the album the band chanced their luck with the old Yardbirds tune 'Think About It' (a Relf/McCartney/Page effort from 1968), and then Tyler himself crooned a tribute to his new baby daughter 'Mia'. It was pleasant enough, but overall more on a par with 'Draw The Line' than either 'Rocks' or 'Toys . . .', and that was something which didn't escape the notice of either the band's fans or the critics.

Nevertheless, a three-month American tour had already been booked to promote the album (tentatively titled the 'Right In The Nuts Tour', as the back cover photo of the band in mine-workers' garb had that particular skit on the LP title painted onto a rock), and time-honoured phrases like 'the show must go on' were beginning to crop up in the Aerosmith vocabulary – or at least their managers'.

Besides, in the latter stages of 'Night In The Ruts' the band had chanced upon a replacement for Joe Perry – the guy had even played the guitar solo on 'Three Mile Smile' (although he was never credited for it) – and that was enough to fire Steven Tyler into wanting to get back on the road, if for no other reason than to prove to Joe Perry that he wasn't indispensable.

The man with the unenviable task of stepping into the six-string hot-spot? Not Derringer axeman Danny Johnson, who the band had considered at one point, nor Schenker who couldn't fulfil the singing requirements Tyler wanted from his sidekick. No, the new 'Smith guitar star was a lesser known mortal by the name of Jimmy Crespo . . .

* * *

Born in Brooklyn, New York, on July 5, 1955, James Crespo Junior struggled through his early years on "The bad side of town" taking a lot of racist abuse for his part-Spanish heritage, turning to music at an early age as it gave him a chance to express himself. His boyhood idols were, predictably, The Beatles, The Stones and The Yardbirds, but by the time he hit his teens he was experiencing some kind of fame himself in a band called Anaconda, "A notorious club band in the New York area."

Crespo's first recording band was Flame, the RCA act managed and produced by Jimmy Iovine, now one of the world's top producers after having

worked with John Lennon, Bruce Springsteen and Simple Minds. Iovine had discovered a sexy girl singer named Marge Raymond and asked Crespo to help write and record some material with her, eventually building the whole band around her. The band ended up doing two albums, 'Flame' (1976) and 'Queen Of The Neighbourhood' (1977), and for a while it looked as though they might make the grade.

"Jimmy was real good at getting people wound up," says Crespo, "and there were a lot of high hopes for Flame. Jimmy also worked with Bruce Springsteen at the time and there was talk of

Bruce throwing a coupla' tunes our way, there was talk of us going on the road with the E-Street Band . . . we thought we were onto a winner."

As it turned out, Flame did "just two three-week tours" opening for Bachman Turner Overdrive in the Midwest ("a totally bizarre experience"), and then for Nektar, once again to no avail. Crespo finally left in 1978 and became a session player, working with Robert Fleichman (who wrote some songs for Journey), Ian Lloyd (on an album produced by Bruce Fairbairn), Helen Schneider, Stevie Nicks "and a bunch of other people I can't remember." But then "for some reason" he got back together with Marge Raymond and wrote some new material for a proposed Flame reunion, attracting the interest of Aerosmith manager David Krebs.

Above: Tyler with new sidekick Jimmy Crespo.

"Nothing seemed to happen though," says Jimmy, "and the idea just died, I guess. Then one day Krebs asked me if I was interested in auditioning for Aerosmith, and as I was bored with just going into a studio day after day playing for other people, I decided to accept the offer.

"So I went down to SIR Studios in New York to meet the band, and they asked me to plug in and play. But I wasn't prepared for the audition at all, and I didn't know the tunes or anything. I tried to learn the tunes as we went along, but I don't think they were impressed with me at all.

"So I left the studio figuring I'd blown it, but I guess they couldn't find anyone else for the job, because a little while later they called me back again – I imagine on Krebs' insistence, although I also knew Tyler's friend Richie Supa from my bar days in New York, and I think he put in a good word for me. Anyway, this time I made sure I learned the tunes before the audition! It went well and the next day Steven called me up and asked me to join the band."

The time was October 1979 and Crespo had two weeks to learn all of Aerosmith's set before the band were due to commence their tour – in between adding touches of guitar work to 'Night In The Ruts'!

"It was all pretty crazy," Jimmy recalls, "but I was really riding high on the buzz at this time."

Little did he or the rest of the band know how futile all the preparation for the tour would be. A secret warm-up date supporting Humble Pie at New York's sleazy Private's nightclub went well enough (although it was so secret hardly anyone turned up – *Superman* actor Christopher Reeve was one of the only interested souls on a sparse dancefloor!). But barely had the trek begun in earnest than Tyler collapsed on-stage at a show in New England, and the rest of the tour was cancelled.

"It was terrible," explained guitarist Rudolph Schenker from support band The Scorpions, "we were just thinking how amazing it was to be opening up for such a great band when that happened. We were very disappointed."

Crespo, meanwhile, was having second thoughts about joining the band. "I was so naïve then I didn't know that Steven's problems were that serious, but the minute the tour had to be pulled I thought, 'Uh-oh, this is not a good sign.' I was doing very well as a studio musician before that, making a good living, and I didn't want my reputation ruined by being part of a band which made the headlines for all the wrong reasons. Once you leave studio work you find there's a stigma attached to you for being part of a band, and I found that after all this Aerosmith stuff happened my phone stopped ringing."

With Aerosmith once again in tatters, Tyler retreated to the squalor of the Gorham Hotel in midtown Manhattan, chosen for its close proximity to Eighth Avenue, Broadway and 42nd Street, where he'd regularly score a couple of $20 bags of 'goodies' from some of the city's seediest drug dealers. He'd hang around the street hoping someone would recognise him – that way he might've got a little extra.

All in all Tyler lived at the Gorham Hotel for a year-and-a-half, his financial situation chronic, his health worse than ever, his wife turning to 'alternative' ways to make money to pay for drugs. According to Tyler, "everything was fine as long as I had my dope and my sugar doughnuts," although one particularly bad cocaine-shooting trip stays with him to this day.

"I had a seizure and woke up on the floor with people banging on my chest. I was in toxic psychosis. I ran into the bathroom and slammed the door. I was totally out of my mind from the coke in my bloodstream. I took a tube of toothpaste and squeezed it into the cracks of the tiles on the wall, because I thought worms and hands were coming in to get me . . ."

Tyler survived that one, but for his next trick he almost pushed his luck too far. After taking his babysitter home on his motorcycle one night, "shit-faced drunk and with a nose full of cocaine," he crashed the bike and, wearing only moccasins at the time, took his heel off in the process. He nearly died, ending up in hospital for six months while all around him friends and, more to the point, business associates, hoped he'd learnt his lesson once and for all.

"Of course I hadn't," he told the author a few years later. "I was just happy to have morphine pumped into me night and day! And then later I'd use the whole thing to get more drugs, limping into the surgery going, 'Hey doc, it feels like the bone's coming through, can I have some Percadans?' I was *really* having a great time by now . . ."

"I remember them supporting Sabbath in '74 — they were a good band then and they are one of the greatest bands in the world now. In fact, I'd say they are one of the best bands ever. They've been through a lot and they've come out on top. And not only that but they are some of the nicest people I've met in this business."
OZZY OSBOURNE

Above: Crespo's former band Flame on the cover of their second album.

CHAPTER SEVEN

GOING...DOWN?

WHILE TYLER SPENT A LARGE part of 1980 recovering from his accident, the rest of the band rehearsed new material at The Wherehouse, sending tapes to the singer for his approval. But as the months slipped by the band's public inactivity (hardly bridged by the release of a 'Greatest Hits' album in October) threw lengthier shadows over their future, and during the summer of 1981 Brad Whitford finally decided it was time he followed Joe Perry's example and walked.

"There wasn't anything going on," said Whitford. "I was getting bored . . ." So he got together with a friend, ex-Ted Nugent vocalist/guitarist Derek St. Holmes, and recorded an album at Axis Studios with producer Tom Allom, wrapping the whole thing up in a fortnight.

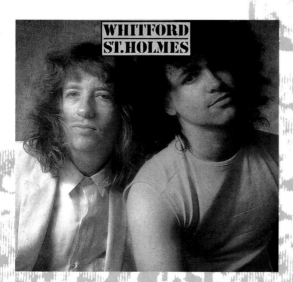

"Then I went back to New York to work with Aerosmith," he explained, "but when I got back nothing was happening. I found it kind of hard to deal with after having completed an album in a couple of weeks with Derek, so I decided to go off and continue working with Derek on a full-time basis."

"We were getting ready to do one of the basic tracks for the album," Tom told *Kerrang!*, "and he (Brad) just called from the airport in Boston saying he wasn't coming – period."

Like Perry's departure, the band blamed the

behaviour of their former colleague on "outside influences" – a thinly veiled reference to spouse interference – but no bitching was going to bring Brad back. With bassist Dave Hewitt and drummer Steve Pace assisting ably, the Whitford/St. Holmes outfit took off around the States to promote their self-titled début album (released in August 1981 on the Columbia label) – a short tour that "kind of fell apart" the minute St. Holmes was lured back into the Nugent camp with the promise of making big bucks. Whitford was left to find solace in California where he did some recording with another friend, US teenybop idol Rex Smith (although despite printing an obligatory 10,000 copies of the album, CBS were forced to burn the lot when the deal fell through). He then accepted an offer from his former partner-in-grime to join The Joe Perry Project for some 20-odd dates in small halls and theatres across America during the Autumn of 1982.

Meanwhile, Aerosmith were faced with the dilemma of choosing a second new guitarist – yet another problem to add to their mounting personnel headaches. It seemed to many of those close to the 'Smiths that maybe the whole episode should be filed under 'sinking ship' and left alone, and even lifelong friends and colleagues like Henry Smith decided it was a ringer for a lost cause.

"The walls were definitely falling in," he told the author. "Jimmy Crespo was a great guitarist, but it clearly wasn't the same without Joe Perry. Steven would be high all the time, but as Crespo didn't 'use' at all – he only drank a little – he wasn't a 'real' member of the band, if you see what I mean. The atmosphere was different and for the crew as well as the band the whole situation felt weird."

"I must admit I was really disappointed when Brad left too," Crespo admitted. "It was nice playing with the original Aerosmith rhythm guitar player because it gave the whole thing a bit of authenticity. When he left though it was like, 'Uh-oh, now this band's *totally* falling apart!' But I was hanging in there because I'd made the decision that I was going to make a record with those guys whatever happened. You know, I'd joined the band, I'd put my reputation on the line, so I thought I should at least put my mark on the project and get something out of it."

In fact, both the band and their management decided they'd soldier on regardless of the indifference of others, and by the Christmas of 1981 a replacement for Whitford had been suggested by Jack Douglas, himself back in the Aerosmith picture after a lengthy absence (in

Left: Whitford goes solo with Derek St Holmes. Right: Rick Dufay, Whitford's replacement.

which he'd produced John Lennon's last album, among others). The man in mind was an old friend of Douglas', a real livewire who he thought might give the band the kick up the pants it required.

Into the fray stepped Richard Marc Dufay.

* * *

On the face of it, Rick Dufay was the perfect substitute for an Aerosmith original – cool, fag-in-mouth looks, arrogant rock star attitude, raunchy low-slung guitar style . . . the epitome of stadium-strutting decadence. But in the confused state in which the band found itself as it hobbled gingerly into 1982, the addition of a certified madman like Dufay was like fighting fire with fire.

"As soon as I joined the band," he told the author, "Steven came up to me and said, 'You're gonna be a stick up my ass, aren't you?', and I said, 'You bet!'"

Rick Dufay was nothing if not a colourful character. From his conception ("I was a bottle of wine on a foggy night in Paris!" – his mother was in France working on the 'Marshall Plan' to rebuild Europe after the war, and had a brief affair with an American actor who was in the *Mrs Miniver* series with Greer Garson – "But no names!"), he was destined to lead a somewhat unorthodox lifestyle, eventually leaving Paris (where he was born on February 19, 1952) to move back to the States with his mother at the age of two.

In New York his mother got a job working for ABC news, and Rick went to live with his grandmother in New Jersey. Then, when he was 12, his mother married an Italian and the family set up home in Englewood, New Jersey, where Rick stayed for five years.

"I remember having a great time at school there," says Rick, "it was all about smoking pot and making protests from what I recall!"

In fact, Rick's claim to schoolboy fame is that he and his friend Billy Proctor managed to get themselves on the cover of a Jimi Hendrix record with one of their protest banners . . .

"Look at the 'Band Of Gypsies' sleeve and you'll see a big 'peace' sign," he still beams with pride. "That's me and my friend holding it!"

Rick left New Jersey for the bright lights of New York City when he was 17, finding himself able to hang out backstage at the Fillmore East rock club as his girlfriend happened to be the daughter of manager Dee Anthony. It was there that the budding musician mixed with the likes of legendary promoter Bill Graham and Frank Barsalona from the Premier Talent booking agency, and these would prove valuable contacts in the future.

Dufay's first bands were numerous and wholly forgettable. The first one of any note, he remembers, was a covers combo called Godspeed who did Pink Floyd, Procol Harum and King Crimson numbers, and lasted about six months. Then in New York he met Humble Pie guitarist Steve Marriott who told him to forget about playing covers and get into playing his own material, so on that advice he spent two years with a band called Modesty Blaise, peddling Edgar Winter/Freddie King-type stuff in the New England

states . . . "anywhere they'd let you do original material."

Eventually, after a brief liaison with another local outfit, Pegasus, Dufay decided to go solo and worked on writing his own songs until he had enough to persuade Bill Graham to manage him. The year was 1977 and Rick had high hopes with the muscle of Graham now behind him, but communication between the two was difficult (Dufay was on the East Coast, Graham on the West) and Graham's commitments with artists more lucrative than Dufay meant little progress was made.

"So I moved to the West Coast in an attempt to get things going," says Rick, "but then Graham said he was off to Egypt with The Grateful Dead for a few months, and I knew then I was wasting my time."

Dufay ultimately changed managers and secured a solo deal with Polydor, making his mark with the 'Tender Loving Abuse' LP in 1980. The producer of the record, the first to be digitally recorded, was none other than Jack Douglas.

"I'd written out a list of 10 producers who I wanted to do the record, and one was Jack," explains Rick. "Then the secretary from my manager's office happened to be on a flight sitting next to this guy who quite obviously fancied her, and he was trying to impress her during his chatting up routine by boasting that he knew Jack Douglas. So this chick goes, 'You know Jack? Great! Can you give this tape to him, we want him to produce this album!'

"So the guy goes over to Jack's house a few days later and throws my tape at him, furious that he didn't even get to ball this chick. He said to Jack, 'All she gave me was this stupid tape!' but Jack really liked the stuff I'd done and called me up."

The pair hooked up in LA during 1979 when Douglas was producing the 'Please Stand By' album for 1994 (the band featuring now ex-LA Jet Karen Lawrence), and formed a mutual admiration society which was to lead to Douglas recommending Dufay for the Aerosmith job. It looked like a golden opportunity for the guitarist after the commercial failure of his solo record, but at first he wasn't quite sure.

"I'd actually met Steven Tyler in the VIP room at The Ritz club in New York a year or so before," he laughs. "I was with Ronnie Wood from The Stones and we were being a bit rowdy, so I guess Steven wondered who this loud-mouthed, obnoxious bastard with a Rolling Stone was. Anyway, a bit later after we'd been eyeing each other up he came over to my table, slammed his elbow down into an arm-wrestling position and said, 'C'mon, let's see who's the strongest here!' It was a pretty macho first meeting!

"But when I eventually went to audition for Aerosmith they weren't a happy unit. They weren't happy with Steven, they weren't happy with their

"I've got so much respect for those guys after what they've been through. And as for Steven Tyler, he's just amazing!"
DAN REED.

GOING...DOWN?

management, they were doing lots of drugs and generally they were a miserable bunch of boys. So I went home afterwards and said to Jack, 'The whole situation sucks, I don't wanna do it'."

Douglas was insistent that he should take the chance though, reasoning that playing to 20,000 people a night with a 'name' band was better than slogging around the clubs on his own, and a subsequent phone call from Joey Kramer finally persuaded Dufay to take the plunge.

"He just said, 'Hey Doof, getcha ass down here, let's get this shit together,' and I kinda fell for the guy. So I went down for another rehearsal and it was a bit better. I still didn't really get on with Jimmy at this time because he just kept himself to himself and we were like black and white, but Tom was a great guy and so was Joey, so I figured it wouldn't be too bad after all."

The main problem for Aerosmith at this point, though, was still Steven Tyler. As with both 'Draw The Line' and 'Night In The Ruts' the simple task of getting the singer to compose a few lyrics was something akin to asking a chimp to philosophise about the state of English literature in the 17th Century, and the months ebbed away frustratingly.

By this time the band had reconvened in Miami, Florida, where they'd rented a house and were working with Jack Douglas on a mobile recording unit which had been pulled up to the building. At Criteria Studios they had laid down a number of ideas, with Crespo the prime mover. There was something entitled 'The Jig Is Up' with Tyler scatting to a jazz influenced beat; there was 'Bolivian Ragamuffin' without the vocals, plus 'Bitches Brew' and 'Joanie's Butterfly' in similar states of undress; and there were primitive versions of 'Jailbait', 'Lightning Strikes', 'Cry Me A River' and another idea which never made the finished album but can be heard on bootlegs that find Tyler ad-libbing nonsensical lyrics.

Indeed, the problem with Tyler became so pronounced during the period in Miami that Tom, Joey and Jimmy eventually got fed up with waiting for him to sober up and left for New York, where 'secret' plans for a new band with ex-Flame singer Marge Raymond were tentatively laid. That left Dufay and an old friend of the band nicknamed 'Brimstone' (Gary Buermele) in Florida to try and straighten the singer out.

"Steven couldn't even write lyrics without falling over," Dufay explained. "So we packed up the truck and moved to the Sonesta Beach Hotel in Miami, where we hoped plenty of rest with nothing but a bit of sunbathing and swimming would get the guy healthy again. But it didn't really work, because we just spent the time drinking and doing some drugs . . .

"In the end I told Krebs I needed help, that Steven needed to go to a clinic and see a doctor . . . but Krebs wasn't interested, he just left it up to me and Brimstone. The feeling from the other guys was, 'We've had enough so it's up to you – good luck!'"

In desperation Dufay and Brimstone got in touch with one of the doctors who'd helped wean Eric Clapton off heroin, and he in turn put them in touch with a methadone clinic which he thought might do the trick. When even that failed they turned to another clinic, where Tyler could get daily vitamin B injections.

"It was a terrible scene," said Dufay. "Steven didn't *wanna* get high, but he just couldn't get straight. We were in Florida for something like four or five months trying to sort Steven out, but we had no help from any of the others. Jimmy Crespo would show his face once in a while, but that was it. It was hopeless, I just sat around doing my quaaludes and cocaine, and Steven was virtually bed-ridden in the state he was in."

Tyler – not to mention Dufay – wasn't to overcome his drug problem for some time yet, but miraculously, recording of 'Rock In A Hard Place' did continue in fits and starts throughout the spring and early summer of 1982 in either Miami or New York's Power Station Studios. It eventually stumbled into the piercing beam of daylight during August like a pot-holer previously lost for months in some dark, dank cave.

Remarkably, the record was a stunner – needle-sharp, knuckle-hard and seemingly suffering little from its fragmented background and extraordinary array of contributors (including three producers – Douglas, Tyler and Tony Bongiovi, second cousin to Jon Bon Jovi – seven assistant engineers, and no less than 11 musicians). In the midst of the controversy surrounding the band's state of mind and body, 'Rock In A Hard Place' was an astonishing statement of misleading sobriety.

On side one alone there was enough to soil the strides of even the most cocksure of contemporaries: 'Jailbait' stuttered with startling staccato-like thrust and Richie Supa's 'Lightning Strikes' crept up behind an eerie, swirling organ intro to punch home with the poisonous power of a brutal back alley gang. Then before you could lick your wounds 'Bitch's Brew' slunk past with a smouldering, slit-eyed stare that mesmerised, before the rasping, rap-headed rauncharama of 'Bolivian Ragamuffin' funked its way into a sozzled saloon bar version of Julie London's 'Cry Me A River' (cut live, according to Crespo).

The flip proved more off-the-wall. 'Rock In A Hard Place (Cheshire Cat)' was a blast with its ballsy, brassy, big-time snazzy-jazzy swing, and 'Jig Is Up' (thirties jazz slang for 'time's up' according to Crespo – "although I didn't know at the time and was too embarrassed to ask Steven!") was a sturdy, snare-trashing stomper that danced like a rat-arsed rhino. But Tyler's 'Push Comes To Shove' was an unusual, bleary late-night singalong with the composer growling in finest Louis Armstrong fashion, and the whole 'Joanie's Butterfly' episode, complete with a weird and whimsical 'Prelude . . .' by Tyler, came shrouded in a mystery that not even the band

floor," panted Xavier Russell in *Sounds*. "'Rock In A Hard Place' could be definitive Aerosmith," gushed a later article on the band, ". . . it showcases their skills as hard rock naturals; scraping solid and fiery riffs plus good humour over 10 well-paced songs, it's nothing short of classic. . .'"

It certainly was a shot in the arm (poor choice of phrase notwithstanding) for American rock, slamming itself bang in the lap of the eighties whilst contemporaries like Nugent and Blue Oyster Cult struggled to shake off the shady stigma of the seventies. Even today in the nineties it sounds exuberantly fresh, the musical equivalent of a snowball down the briefs.

Years later Tyler was to cite 'Rock In A Hard Place' as one of his favourite Aerosmith albums, and even Joe Perry admitted dismay at not being able to record 'Lightning Strikes'. Dufay, who only contributed the odd guitar part here and there, also still rates the record highly some eight years

Above: Tyler gets the shakes.
Right: Jimmy Crespo.
Bottom right: Rick Dufay.

could untangle afterwards.

"I wanted that track to be an instrumental," Crespo explains, "because I imagined it as being like one of Jimmy Page's acoustic pieces. But Steven was insistent that it should have lyrics, because he'd had some kind of brainstorm as to what it should all be about. Even today I'm still confused about what it actually means . . ."

With words like 'hooved' wafting to the surface many thought the song recounted Tyler's first meeting with the devil, whereas the singer claimed it was a dream he'd had about a unicorn Pegasus. Whether it was a bad acid trip or a pretentious attempt at abstract poetry, few got the joke when word filtered through that a Joanie's Butterfly was in fact a sex aid!

Despite the absence of Perry and Whitford (the latter contributing only rhythm guitar to 'Lightning Strikes'), 'Rock In A Hard Place' was well received by the press, particularly in Britain, and was a certified triumph for Jimmy Crespo, who'd written the music for six of the nine original tracks (co-writing both the title track and 'Joanie's Butterfly' with Jack Douglas).

"As soon as the stylus hit the wax it melted, and my speaker covers blew across the living room

on, and Crespo, whose baby it really was, says ''I liked the album, but unfortunately there was a lot of drama around the album which took something away from my enjoyment of it.''

As far as the powers-that-be behind Aerosmith were concerned though, the fact that they'd managed to wring an album out of an extremely disorientated band was an achievement on its own, and the combined forces of Leber-Krebs and CBS immediately set to work on promotional ideas for the record. The album's sleeve, a stupid Stonehenge snap that served only to further Aerosmith's affinity with the soon-to-be-released *Spinal Tap* heavy metal parody film, was hardly

the kind of thing to entice the more discerning punter. So a scam was hatched to film a video in 3-D . . . a 'brainwave' thought so brilliant by CBS that they funded three of the buggers – 'Bolivian Ragamuffin', 'Bitch's Brew' and, oddly, 'Sweet Emotion' – as well as the conventional video the band had shot for the single, 'Lightning Strikes' (which had them togged up in street gang garb, hair slicked back an' all!). At first it was even whispered that the 3-D footage would be sent out with a trailer for the new *Jaws III* flick . . .

''The whole 3-D thing was crazy,'' laughs Dufay. ''To get the effect you had to have the special 3-D glasses, but it wasn't that cool. It cost a fortune, it was a total waste of time . . . and we were all out of our trees at the time anyway. There was a big promotional 'do' for the videos at Studio 54 in New York, but I don't think they even saw the light of day . . .''

Back on planet Earth the more serious business of heaving the hefty expanse of Aerosmith flesh back onto the road had begun in earnest. Rehearsals had been kick-started at Private's in New York – a three-floored club with a lounge on one level, a dancefloor on another and a big stage in a large room at the top – and straight away the Tyler/Dufay confrontation started to cause friction.

''Steven pulled me to one side one day,'' says Dufay. ''We did a coupla lines of blow (cocaine) and then he proceeded to give me a lecture on the meaning of life, and what it was really like to be in Aerosmith. He was really testing me out – like, 'You're gonna flip in front of 30,000 people, man!' – to see if I could deal with it all. He was so nervous about the tour and he was trying to scare me. I was OK at first, but the more he went on

Bottom (left to right): Geddy Lee of Rush, Jimmy Crespo, Stevie Ray Vaughan, tennis star Vitas Gerulitas, Tom Hamilton and Steven Tyler at the 'Tennis Rock' bash at The Pier, New York, August 1983. Right: (left to right): Tyler, Gerulitas, John McEnroe and Tom Hamilton. Far right: Tyler with Buddy Guy.

about it I started to think, 'Oh shit, maybe I *am* gonna flip out!'''

After some time at Private's, Aerosmith hauled their full stage set to the Concorde 1200-seater hall in New Hampshire, where according to Dufay they rehearsed for two months . . . in between parties. Finally, the 'Rock In A Hard Place' tour was thrown into first gear during the autumn and winter, and while some US fans saw the new Aerosmith as a 'fake', thousands still flocked to the shows every night.

''The first gig in New Hampshire was amazing,''

this thing work is if Steven has an ally, because the one thing that bugs him is that he's forever having people put him down for getting high. Whereas if I'm getting high with him he's got a partner in crime, and he'll feel better towards the band'.''

It was a warped way of looking at it, but it seemed to work for a while.

''I was the middle man really,'' adds Rick. ''I'd keep Tom and Joey together with Steven. I'd go into Steven's dressing room and make sure he was cool, then I'd go into Tom and Joey's dressing room and check them out too. I was like the manager of the band back then, I guess!''

On-stage things were beginning to gel reasonably well too. Supported by the likes of Pat Travers, Rose Tattoo, Kix, Bryan Adams (then on his first tour) and Dio, the band wound their way across the States during 1983 with a set that left nothing to chance: the now-essential *Psycho* theme would open the floodgates for 'Back In The Saddle', and there then followed a set of mostly old material like 'Lord Of The Thighs', 'Lick And A Promise', 'Sweet Emotion' and 'Walk This Way', with only 'Lightning Strikes' and the title track

"Aerosmith are the ultimate in honest, gutsy rock 'n' roll. Of that there's no doubt."

ANDY MITCHELL, TORANAGA

Dufay beamed on a visit to London in 1987. ''I loved every minute of it – falling all over the place and stealing the spotlight from Crespo.

''Basically what I did in Aerosmith was light a fire under Steven's ass. At first Steven got really pissed off with me stealing all the reviews. I mean, he'd get on the plane in the morning, read the papers and go, 'What's all this Dufay shit? He's supposed to be the sleeper in the band!' I mean, I'd get fired by Steven God knows how many times, but I'd always go, 'Fine, see ya . . .' and Steven would go, 'Where ya going, can't I get mad at you sometimes?'''

As the trek unwound, Tyler and Dufay gradually formed a closer bond – one which internal observers knew was potentially lethal, related as it was, inevitably, to their common ground of habitual drug use.

''Steven and I got along great after a while,'' says Rick today, ''because although Steven and Jimmy had a great writing partnership, Jimmy didn't get high with Steven – he'd only drink wine, and therefore he wasn't that much fun to be with. Whereas I'd always be getting high with Steven . . . and I'd get high with Tom and Joey too. At first I thought Tom and Joey saw me as trouble, hanging out with Steven and getting him high all the time. But early on I went up to them and said, 'Hey listen man, the only way we're gonna make

flying the flag from the new 'Rock In A Hard Place'.

''We did some great gigs and we did some awful gigs,'' says Dufay, ''depending on how screwed up we all were – especially Steven. What made it great though was the sense of the unexpected, because we just didn't know if Steven was gonna make it through the show or not, and I think that tension is kinda cool in a rock 'n' roll band.

''We had a guy in the crew called Rich Goulberty, and we had a system of hand signals for when we thought Steven was on the verge of keeling over . . . like, 'Whoa Rich, he's gonna go!', and Rich would dash on-stage and catch the guy as he was teetering!''

''It was a pretty gruelling job, it really knocked the crap out of you,'' says Rich, who started out as head of security for the band before ending up as one of their tour managers. ''It was a very neurotic, very chaotic job, because I was responsible for everything they got up to. I basically had to make sure they stayed alive, which wasn't easy!

''The main thing was keeping an eye on Steven all the time, making sure he didn't go too far overboard. We didn't have the authority to stop him doing drugs, because that wasn't really the fashion in the early eighties. But we did try to stop drugs reaching him, and our biggest problem there was keeping fans away from him before the show, because if they got to him they figured the way to be cool and hang out with the guy was to give him some dope. What they didn't realise was that they were only sabotaging their own evening, because Steven would go on-stage wrecked and collapse. I remember that happening at the Worcester Centrum in Massachusetts, when we had to carry the poor guy off stage after a couple of numbers.''

Libellous rumour has it that Joe Perry had turned up to that show and offered his old pal some heroin, which Tyler proceeded to shoot by way of showing off. But it was never proved. Anyway . . .

''Carrying Steven got to be a real speciality of mine,'' laughs Rich. ''Sometimes we'd arrive at airports and I'd have to carry him over my shoulder 'cos he'd be out cold. I'd get to the desk and the guy would go, pointing to Steven, 'Are you gonna check that bag in or are you gonna carry it on!' And then people would come up to me and ask if he was dead, there'd be people taking pictures of me carrying him . . . y'know, it was like a freak show.

''And God forbid we ever had to make an early morning flight! I'd try to get him up in the morning and he'd go mad, throwing food and furniture at me, so I'd throw it back and there'd be a wild fight at the hotel. After all that I'd have to pack all his stuff up and carry him to the next gig myself. You know, sometimes we wished we could've just packed Steven in a giant flight case and checked him into the baggage hold (an idea used recently for the band's video of 'The Other Side' single)!

''Actually, there were times when we thought he was gonna die,'' Rich adds, adopting a more serious tone, ''and a few times he nearly did. I'd have to smack him around a little when he partied too much, when he was dancing a little too close to the edge. I had to get physical and it wasn't nice because I loved the guy, still do, and we didn't need all that bullshit. He was a lovely guy and a great talent, but he had a real big problem and it was dragging him towards an early demise every day.''

''The whole atmosphere at this time was very strained,'' says Crespo, ''and a lot of people were getting really pissed off at the state Steven was in, they felt he was screwing up their careers. There was a lot of animosity at this point and people were leaving almost every day. The tension was hard to cut through . . .''

And Dufay's wacky attempt to keep the singer in check by being some sort of partner-in-poison was backfiring drastically too.

''Rick was totally out of his mind,'' says Rich. ''One time we were on a flight to Hawaii and he

Above: Tyler and Crespo.
Right: Rick Dufay.

decided he was going to jump out of the aeroplane. He was out of his head after doing too many drugs, not sleeping for a couple of days and generally just trying to deal with the pressures of being in the band. It was pretty scary. A few of us had to hold him down and sit on him, 'cos he would've opened the door and we would've all gone!''

In the midst of the madness there were some

great shows to savour, though. One was the *Superbowl Of Rock*, staged over April 23 and 24, 1983, at the Miami baseball stadium and the Tangerine Bowl in Florida. Over 200,000 fans saw Aerosmith appear as 'special guests' to Journey on a bill that also featured Bryan Adams and Sammy Hagar, and although it was a bit humiliating for the 'Smiths to have to appear second on the bill to someone again, Rich Goulberty recalls them ''digging deep into their bag of tricks to blow everyone else off that day!''

Photographer Ross Halfin remembers the show for another reason though – Tyler taking a huge gulp of Jack Daniel's mid-set and then dashing to the side of the stage to vomit over the feet of Journey's manager Herbie Herbert – so let's just say that the band still weren't choirboy-clean even on their better days!

Aerosmith stayed on the road in America and Canada throughout 1983, careering into 1984 like an off-course fireball. The tour hadn't bombed, but it clearly wasn't the same without Perry and Whitford. The fans knew it, the critics knew it, so did Tyler, and as if to rub it in further, the estranged guitarists showed up backstage at the band's Valentine's Day show at the Orpheum Theater in Boston. The graffiti was on the wall . . .

Before that the band had tried to get some new material together for their next album. Crespo had a tune in mind, Hamilton and Dufay had one, and Dufay had one of his own entitled 'Written In Stone' (which he still hopes to release one day). Basic tracks had been laid down in a New Jersey studio, and then the band went into the Record Plant with engineer Lee DeCarlo to do some overdubs, but all this time the task of motivating Tyler to write some lyrics was proving impossible.

''It was over, man,'' says Dufay. ''It was like beating a dead horse. The thing between Steven and Jimmy wasn't firing, Tom and Joey were fed up . . . the whole thing sucked.''

''We just couldn't get Steven going,'' Crespo explains. ''Deep down he wanted Joe Perry back, and he'd talk to me about the guy all the time. It'd be like, 'Joe did this, Joe did that, Joe did it this way . . .' Eventually I accepted that the only way Aerosmith would work again would be if Joe and Brad returned, because that's how Steven wanted it.''

''In the end,'' adds Dufay, ''even *I* wanted Steven and Joe to get back together. One night Steven, his girlfriend Teresa (Barrick, now his wife), Rich Goulberty and me an' my missus went over to the Bottom Line Club in New York to see The Joe Perry Project. We went backstage and I said to Steven and Joe, 'Hey, I think it's time you two guys got back together.' So Steven's going, 'What do you mean? It's not your place to say that!', because he had to be macho and not let Joe know he needed him. David Krebs was really mad at me for suggesting that idea to them, but they obviously thought about it afterwards . . .''

CHAPTER EIGHT

BACK IN THE SADDLE

TWO MONTHS AFTER JOE Perry and Brad Whitford showed their faces at Aerosmith's Valentine's Day gig, word of a reconciliation was in the air, and in April, 1984, an official announcement was duly made to the effect that the best-loved Aerosmith line-up was to reunite.

For Tyler and Hamilton the news was a massive relief, and even Kramer had come round to the idea, although he'd initially said he wouldn't play with Perry again because he felt Joe stabbed Aerosmith in the back by leaving the band in the first place.

Crespo and Dufay, meanwhile, slipped off into the shadows. Crespo went on to play with another Krebs artist, Adam Bomb, before taking a two-year break in LA to "clear out the cobwebs and rid my life of drugs and alcohol." After marrying Cynthia and starting a family, he did session work with the likes of sixties star Bonnie Bramlett's group Bandaloo Doctors and, more recently, Billy Squier. He's currently working on a couple of projects which he hopes will come to fruition sometime during 1991.

As for Rick Dufay, his main task was also to get himself straight once and for all, and after years of jumping on and falling off the wagon (a faltering solo project the result of fluctuating fortunes), he finally seems to be pulling through. A solo album recorded for the Paris-based Link label appears to have been scrapped, but Rick now has a nifty (albeit unnamed) five-piece band together in LA and is looking for a deal at the time of going to press.

Back in the balmy, buoyant spring of 1984, it came to light that the driving force behind the reformation of Aerosmith was Tim Collins, a Boston promoter who'd taken over the management of The Joe Perry Project from another local promoter Don Law who'd replaced The JPP's first managers, Leber-Krebs. Collins and partner Steve Barrasso secured The Project a recording contract with MCA after their liaison with Columbia fizzled out, but just as Perry was getting ready to record 'Once A Rocker . . .' for MCA, the label's management changed and new boss Irving Azoff made it clear he'd have no time for The JPP.

Perry was sleeping on Collins' couch at the time, having split from wife Elissa and lost almost everything but his guitar in the settlement. Things were so desperate that the strung-out guitarist even considered a position in Alice Cooper's backing band.

After all, The Project had deteriorated from selling 250,000 copies of their first album to shifting only 40,000 of their third. The job of managing Joe Perry had become "a very expensive habit" for Collins whose own drug consumption, he has since admitted, was also dangerously high. Both agreed it was time something changed.

Relations between Perry and Tyler had cooled somewhat by now. In fact, JPP singer Mach Bell remembers a gig in Salisbury Beach, Massachusetts, when "the whole band (Aerosmith), except for Hamilton, jammed with us on-stage." Bell also claims he thought Perry and Tyler would never work together again, as Perry had already begun writing with Alice Cooper. But Tim Collins realised something was afoot after The JPP's Country Club gig in LA, when Perry asked his manager if he knew where Tyler was . . .

Tyler was in fact in Florida and the two conversed politely on the phone for hours. Tyler told Perry he couldn't believe he was considering playing with Alice Cooper; Perry defended his decision (he'd already written six songs with Alice) but realised deep down it wasn't the shrewdest of career moves.

"That was kind of the first night the wall broke down," Collins told *RIP*. "It was the first night he (Perry) got serious about a reunion."

When Perry did get serious about a reunion, however, there was a mind-boggling maze of complicated contractual problems to negotiate. Perry was already in the process of suing Leber-Krebs (ultimately successfully, for neglect of legal commitments) which raised the sensitivity of the situation to dramatic proportions, eventually unleashing a tornado of furious lawsuits which aggravated matters almost beyond salvation.

With Leber-Krebs out of the picture at Perry's insistence, the Collins/Barrasso organisation assumed management responsibilities for the reformed Aerosmith which now included Brad Whitford who had signed up again. Collins' first task was to clear a path through the tunnel of legal obstacles for the re-born band to see daylight

Right: "Aaaarrgh!!" Tyler welcomes Perry back into the fold.

again.

In Boston the group rehearsed garage-style at a Howard Johnson's hotel. To play shows with the lawsuits outstanding might invite additional claims from Leber-Krebs – including the potential seizure of box office takings – but Collins knew it was essential to get them back on the road as soon as possible, both to focus their energies into something positive and to raise some much-needed cash. But . . .

"The band were still signed to Columbia," Collins told *Rolling Stone*, "and no one at Columbia would speak to us. They would only speak to Leber-Krebs, who had a production contract for, like, seven more records."

So Collins threw a middle finger in the direction of Columbia and, with financial help from the Monterey Peninsula Artists company, whacked the band out on the road in an attempt to get them out of their contract one way or another. He invented a bogus corporation for each show so that the box-office takings could not be claimed by creditors. "They'd try to attach the box office for Aerosmith, but there'd be no Aerosmith," he explained. It was brilliant.

But the grief wasn't over yet. Promoters who'd been burnt before by the band's notorious unreliability, a reputation matured into legend by their much-publicised musical and physical decline, had to be persuaded to reinvest in the reactivated monster called Aerosmith. The tour, Collins commented later, was turning into "guerilla warfare."

Nevertheless Aerosmith were 'Back In The Saddle', and the 70-date tour of the same name thundered across America in a fit of well-intended aural malice. With Orion The Hunter (featuring ex-Boston singer/guitarist Brad Delph) in support, the band toured from June to August, returning after a short break (during which new material was written) to stay on the road until January of the following year.

But although Aerosmith had decided they'd straighten themselves out for the tour, old habits reared their ugly heads with depressing inevitability, culminating in another demonstration of 'gravity on the unstable man' at a show in Springfield, Illinois, where Tyler finished up hoarse and horizontal. The show was cancelled and Collins tried to arrange sending free copies of the 'Greatest Hits' album to every disappointed punter.

"I didn't want to hurt their reputation any more than it was," Collins explained. "We almost got arrested that night, but we talked our way out of that."

Collins was indeed proving himself rather good at the 'gift of the gab' game – fighting a rearguard action against the exocet lawsuits while still managing to go on the offensive looking for a new record deal. When Columbia finally released Aerosmith from the chains of their contract it turned out that Collins had been courting the attention of Geffen Records in the meantime. John Kalodner, the head of A&R at Geffen, had quite a reputation for picking up the bones of stumbling seventies stars and dressing them up for the eighties, and although that old blast from the past Clive Davis – now boss of the Arista label – also expressed interest in signing (or re-signing) the band, Collins decided Geffen would be the best bet.

"I just thought they were one of the greatest American rock bands ever," said Kalodner, an eccentric cross between John Lennon during his

Top right: Tyler and Perry with Run DMC on the set of the video shoot for their joint hit single 'Walk This Way'.
Bottom right: The confusing 'backwards' sleeve for the 'Done With Mirrors' album.

hippy period and Catweazle with a hernia. ''If someone could work with them on their music, they could make great records again.''

Chosen to help craft Aerosmith's 'comeback' album into something viable for the mid-eighties was Ted Templeman, a much respected American producer probably best known for his work on six Van Halen albums.

''We were looking around at possible producers,'' Tyler told Malcolm Dome of *Kerrang!* at the time, ''when we heard that Teddy really wanted to work with us. He appeared at the Grammy awards in Los Angeles earlier this year (1985) to pick up some prizes and was asked which band he'd most like to get involved with, and his answer was Aerosmith.''

''At the time,'' added Perry, ''other names had cropped up. For instance George Martin, who worked with us on the 'Sgt. Pepper . . .' soundtrack, was mentioned as a possibility to record with us in Montserrat, but we were not very happy with that idea. So Ted came as a breath of fresh air.''

Templeman went to see Aerosmith play at the Spectrum in Philadelphia, and impressed the band afterwards with his ''attitude and outlook.'' He told

them he thought they'd never been properly captured on vinyl before, the band agreed meekly, and so with Templeman at the helm they set about putting that right at Fantasy studios in Berkeley, California, during July.

Tyler and Perry had actually prepared a whole album's worth of material – and more – within a month, before hooking up with Templeman. Bursting with new ideas and electrified by new-found enthusiasm, they had rattled through ''something like one song per day'' in their keenness to impress, and spent the first two days at Fantasy with Templeman just running through the numbers with all tape machines off to give the producer a 'feel' for the material. What they didn't know, however, was that Templeman was secretly recording everything, and many of those first takes ended up on the final vinyl.

''It was his way of getting a live ambience into the sound,'' laughed Tyler. ''He'd actually had his engineer, Jeff Hendrickson, working hard on getting the right mixing desk levels before we'd arrived . . . which meant we just relaxed and let rip.''

They did too, not least on a new version of 'Let The Music Do The Talking', which Perry had written before leaving Aerosmith, taking it with him when he walked. The band had slipped it in their set on the 'Back In The Saddle' tour, and it had become a song synonymous with the patched-up

Tyler/Perry partnership.

"I used to look across the stage when Jimmy Crespo was in the band and somehow it just didn't feel right," Tyler had said. "I did miss Joe . . ."

"I had a similar experience with The Joe Perry Project," Joe admitted. "I just couldn't find a singer with whom I hit it off the way Steven and I always did."

And Perry had always wondered how 'Let The Music . . .' would sound with the voice he'd always intended it for, belting out its sensible sentiments.

It sounded great, and so did 'My Fist Your Face', crunching in immediately after and rolling along like a freight train on a skateboard. That track in particular was quintessential Aerosmith, a smouldering, smoke-in-your-eyes riff, big boot-up-the-backside drums and a drooling line in loose-tongued lyrics that breathed pure back alley grime. Goosebump City. The business . . .

Elsewhere, Tyler and Perry seemed to flirt between the Zeppelin-shaded area of their creativity bank, and the good old bash-it-out/tattier-than-a-tramp-in-a-tank-top approach which had served them so well in the past. 'Shame On You', for example, brandished a stop-start funk-junk riff that might've inspired a Page/Plant opus a few years before, and 'She's On Fire' possessed obvious Zeppelinesque qualities, plodding menacingly on the dark side of a slide-guitar grunge with the faintest wafts of Eastern promise

kissing the grooves.

'Gypsy Boots' was a more straight-down-the-line affair, a breathless belt with gut-twisting gusto, and 'The Hop' which wrapped the record up wasn't far behind in the race, bleating with heavy harmonica as it galloped for glory. But 'The Reason A Dog' and 'Sheila' weren't quite in the same unruly class, and overall the album shaped up like a pint of well-known lager: it was good . . . but not that good.

Entitled 'Done With Mirrors', the record was completed in August at the Record Plant in New York, emerging in November 1985 with a literally backward marketing campaign to back it up. The cover of the record, including the inner bag and even the label, had been deliberately printed back-to-front as a gimmick, an idea all five band members later denounced.

It received good reviews all the same, and the tour announced to promote it proved a reasonable commercial success. But the album didn't sell as well as everyone had hoped – barely moving 400,000 copies when all but 'Rock In A Hard Place' before it had reached platinum status.

"I wasn't too happy with a lot of the things that went down with the 'Done With Mirrors' album,"

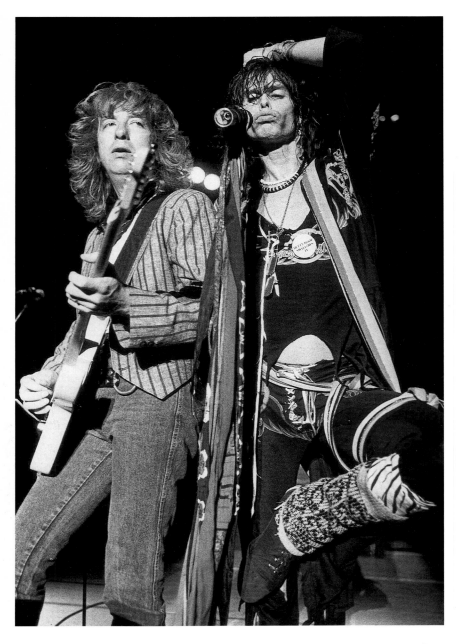

Tyler told the author shortly after its release. "So much of that album sounds undone to me; I wasn't happy with the middle section of 'The Reason A Dog', I wasn't too pleased about certain other bits . . . it just wasn't the best we could've made it. I mean, we didn't even put 'Darkness' on the record (the single the 'Smiths released in the US, backed by live versions of 'My Fist . . .' and 'The Hop') – that's how screwed up we were!"

"When it wasn't a big seller it really kicked us in the pants," said Brad, "because we were stupid enough to believe we could spit onto a piece of vinyl and it would sell."

"It was a real awakening," added Tom. "It proved how we must've taken our fans for granted."

Just before the release of '. . . Mirrors'

FIFTY EIGHT

Aerosmith undertook a series of eight outdoor festival dates in the US dubbed 'The Preview Tour', during which they'd aired some of their new material for the first time. At one show in Phoenix, headlined by new Leber-Krebs act The Scorpions, David Krebs spent the entire day trying to avoid Aerosmith, much to be the band's amusement. But touring began in earnest in January 1986, Ted Nugent falling into place as opening act, just like the old days.

The tour was originally going to be worldwide, taking in Europe and Japan (where they still weren't sure of a warm welcome from the promoter, after the 'turkey' episode in 1977). But as was so often the case in the past, the North American/Canadian continent hogged the band to itself.

The 'DWM' shows were, on the whole, a certified success, even though Aerosmith attracted little more than dyed-in-the-wool devotees (albeit by the thousand). They'd been away a long time, and the kids on the corner of each block read magazines full of new rock bands to talk about, dress like and get rid of their dandruff to: Motley Crue, Ratt, even Guns n' Roses were beginning to poke their snotty noses into the picture, picking up a wild reputation for an even wilder cover of 'Mama Kin', which had become a regular in their repertoire.

But Aerosmith still had more serious problems to deal with. The end of the '. . . Mirrors' tour was cancelled in May with the band in pathetic physical shape. Tyler's liver, he was repeatedly advised, was on its last legs – and his heroin problem was no walk in the park either. Perry was also no slouch in the drug abuse stakes, Hamilton had a severe cocaine dependency, Kramer and Whitford were raving alcoholics . . . the whole band was rotten to the core.

Tim Collins, who'd recently sorted out his own drug problem, had tried to drag the health of his boys back from the brink before, but he'd failed, complaining . . . "You can lead a horse to water, but you can't make it drink." Making Aerosmith drink wasn't a problem, *stopping* them was something different. So Collins gave the band an ultimatum: shape up or ship out. "We had to choose between the drugs and the music," said Perry. They chose the music . . .

. . . But not before Collins and the band confronted their singer separately about his personal problem, fearing that he was so close to death that he might not make it if he didn't take action, like, NOW.

"I'm still a little bitter about that," Tyler confessed later, "because there were guys in the room that day who had problems of their own telling *me* how screwed up *I* was." Nevertheless . . .

"I knew I had to do something. I wanted to confront my addiction, so for a period of a month I went every night to a course in Boston of a psychological nature. There I was effectively humiliated by being asked publicly to recall the times when I'd made an asshole of myself in front of friends and couldn't stand up long enough to carry through a show. The treatment made me realise things about myself and forced a change of attitude.''

Tyler was told that his treatment would be wasted if he was just going to go back to ''a bunch of guys who were still doing drugs,'' so it was agreed that everyone within the Aerosmith organisation would clean up together. Through a friend, Collins had discovered The Caron Foundation in Pennsylvania, a rehabilitation centre with a decent track record, and there Aerosmith's chemical confusions were dissolved slowly and painfully, but surely.

Behind the rehab triumph was the 12-step programme, a universal method of treatment for alcoholics which involves a laborious process of self-discipline and spiritual awakening.

The 12 steps are as follows:
1. Admitting that you're addicted, that alcohol is your God and that you're powerless against it.
2. Admitting that there is a power greater than yourself (i.e. God).
3. Turning to God for help, thereby accepting religion as part of life.
4. Admitting all your faults and negative feelings, and making a list of them.
5. Confessing your faults to a church minister, somebody already in the 'fellowship', etc.
6. Preparing yourself to allow God to remove those defects of character.
7. Asking God to remove all your shortcomings.
8. Compiling a list of those people you have harmed in the past.
9. Making direct amends with those people, except when to do so would cause further harm to those or others.
10. Continuing to act like a Christian in everyday life.
11. Keeping in constant contact with God through prayer and meditation.
12. Passing the word, loving thy neighbour and upkeeping all Christian values.

When Aerosmith finally came out of the alcoholic and chemical stupor they'd been in for over 10 years, they focused their bleary eyes with mild disbelief on their new-found status as pop kings. It was late 1986 and the precocious New York rappers who called themselves Run DMC had covered 'Walk This Way' for their 'Raising Hell' album, notching up a huge international hit with the track when it was released as a single.

Tyler and Perry had in fact helped out with the 'hip hop' remake on the suggestion of producer Rick Rubin, a big noise behind the mixing desk in the Big Apple who'd helped establish the Def Jam label at the forefront of the burgeoning rap movement. Why, they'd even been coaxed into cameo roles for the song's MTV-obliging video . . . and what if the other three weren't too chuffed at being left out? It was just a bit of fun . . .

''We did the song in five hours,'' Perry told the author on the phone at the time, ''and I think Steven and I both enjoyed the final result.'' He went on to praise the racially-integrated rock/rap crossover that was widening both Aerosmith's and Run DMC's audience ('Raising Hell' went double

platinum just like an Aerosmith album of old!), but he stressed that the rap thing was a one-off, adding: ''The only scratching I do is with my guitar up against my amplifier!''

'Walk This Way' got to number four in the States and even took Aerosmith into the Top 10 in Britain (reaching number eight in September 1986). The video, with Tyler back-flipping and show-stealing like an MC mutha from hell, got heavy rotation on MTV and widespread exposure in the UK on pop programmes like the BBC's *Top Of The Pops* and ITV's *The Chart Show*, effectively planting little seeds of that Aerosmith magic right into the living rooms of those who'd never have let them through the front door otherwise.

It was a marketing masterstroke, perfectly timed, perfectly executed and producing a perfect result. And it would've been even better had it been planned.

CHAPTER NINE

A SIGHT FOR SORE EYES

AND SO IT WAS WITH CLEAR heads and much more familiar faces that Aerosmith headed up to Little Mountain Sound Studios in Vancouver, Canada, to start work on their next album with producer Bruce Fairbairn in the spring of 1987. Initial attempts to get the album started had been made during February by Rick Rubin, with whom the band enjoyed a keen friendship after the 'Walk This Way' episode, and a total of six song ideas were duly demoed – including the titles 'Love Me Like A Birdog' (reputedly the embryonic 'Dude (Looks Like A Lady)'), 'One Time', 'Take It Easy' and 'Hollywood' – judging by the tapes all very basic rockers.

Rubin, however, had several other projects packed into his schedule at this time (including a Slayer album and a Run DMC film to pursue), and couldn't afford to spend six months in the studio with Aerosmith. Fairbairn took over and never looked back.

Suddenly, Aerosmith's popularity had blossomed again; everyone wanted to work with them, everyone wanted to talk to them, everyone WANTED them again. To cash in on the reunion Columbia released a patchwork of old live tapes (some 'touched up' by Crespo and Adam Bomb) called 'Classics Live' in April 1986, which included the previously unreleased studio version of 'Major Barbra' as an added bonus. While the band were hard at work on their new studio effort, the suitably-titled sequel 'Classic Live II' was pushed out in June, this time with the band themselves contributing personal live tapes from over the years to ensure it would be better than the first affair, which was largely cobbled together by David Krebs.

By August Aerosmith had their own spanking new platter to parade, its title – 'Permanent Vacation'. As the first drug-free record the band had ever attempted it was a sharp and disciplined effort, commercially enhanced by Geffen's decision to bring in the hottest hit-writers of the time – Jim Vallance, Holly Knight and Desmond Child, rock's version of Stock, Aitken and Waterman, who'd penned hits for Bryan Adams, Kiss, Cher, Bon Jovi and a slew of others between

them. The finished product was polished, packaged and promoted with the kind of uncompromising professionalism needed to compete in the late eighties.

Aerosmith had arrived in the new era, with Kalodner steering the ship and a worldwide rock audience as a welcoming committee. Radio had been cleverly catered for, MTV was duly pandered to with slick, snappy videos shot for the singles 'Dude (Looks Like A Lady)', 'Angel' and 'Rag Doll' with 'happening' director Marty Callner (another of Kalodner's cronies), and the whole Aerosmith machine was retuned and refuelled for modern mobilisation. Even the old band logo was dug up and dusted down after some concerned souls – not least Joe Perry – attributed the failure of 'Done With Mirrors' partly to the absence of the famous 'Smith insignia.

The record itself was a concoction of traditional Aerosmith sass and sleaze with a commercial cutting edge. Tracks like openers 'Heart's Done Time' and 'Magic Touch' still cranked with wicked guitars and piledriving drums, but now there were soft centres within the steel-hard shells, and Fairbairn's pristine production contrived to make the most of the more melodic qualities of Tyler's voice.

It also appeared that the policy for 'Permanent Vacation' was to leave no stone in the band's

"They are the epitome a hard rock band that maintains groove and soul. Steven Tyler is a genius and totally phenomenal. They we the first band I ever listened to and 'Drea On' was the first rock song I ever got into."
TOMMY CARADONNA, ALICE COO BAND

spectrum of influences unturned, to cover all bases with a song for every taste bud. 'Rag Doll' was rife with a rag-time jazz groove that called for a five-piece horn section, 'Simoriah' had a strange sixties-like appeal with even a touch of The Monkees in the guitar riff, and a climactic cover of The Beatles' 'I'm Down' served as another acknowledgement to the musical birthplace of the band.

Elsewhere, 'Girl Keeps Coming Apart' also summoned The Margarita Horns (including Fairbairn on trumpet) to add a brassy backbone to the uptempo party-time parade, the bluesy 'Hangman Jury' croaked with real rocking-chair-on-the-veranda authenticity, 'St. John' shuffled with finger-clicking R&B cool, 'Angel' sobbed with

archetypal big-ballad emotion and instrumental finale 'The Movie' throbbed with a dark, mysterious mood that Tyler later described as an attempt at "guided imagery."

Finally there were the two out 'n' out rockers, primed with the kind of bar-room brilliance that Aerosmith could almost call their own by now. 'Permanent Vacation', a Tyler/Whitford gem, came complete with steel drums, all manner of sound effects and a harpoon-like hook that would've landed Jaws. And 'Dude . . .', the fella-in-a-frock fracas that Tyler later hinted was a true story, was like a riot on the Reeperbahn, instantly installing itself in the memory as an Aerosmith classic.

'Permanent Vacation' was in fact a comprehensive triumph for the 'new' Aerosmith. Its diversity shattered preconceptions and banished the blinkers of the narrow-minded, its subtleties and complexities surprised even the faithful, and its maturity proved that life could indeed begin at 40 for the born-again band. Such sobriety and new-found awareness even extended to a highly commendable 'Save The Whales – Support Greenpeace' note on the sleeve – sound effects from two killer whales from the Vancouver Aquarium having been used on the intro to 'Heart's Done Time'. And this from a band who years earlier had been the personification of hell-raising rock 'n' roll decadence!

A month after the album's release, Steven Tyler and Joe Perry headed for Europe on a promotional tour that was to include a face-to-face

"Actually, Aerosmith are responsible for everything that's going on in Los Angeles right now."

FRANK STEELE, FASTER PUSSYCAT

with the traditionally hostile British press for the first time in 10 years. This time though talk was of an album that had been almost universally praised, and of a band who were cleaner than a vicar's tea party. Tyler in particular rose to the occasion by conducting a startlingly frank and revealing interview with the author at the old WEA offices in Soho's Broadwick Street. It was a brave gesture by a man desperate to exorcise his horrific past in public, and for the first time the full extent of the extraordinary rise, fall and rise of Aerosmith was painstakingly disclosed.

"I started taking drugs when I was 16 because it was the natural thing for anyone growing up in the States, or certainly in my home town, to do," Tyler confessed. "Then it got to the stage where I'd drink an eight-ounce glass of Jack Daniel's and fill my nose up with cocaine before I went on stage, and I'd be flying, man.

"I once had three Porsches and I sold them all so I could snort up half of Peru. I was paying $1000 a gramme for heroin, and doing about three-to-five grammes a week. I mean, I would've traded my nuts in for a good ounce of heroin in them days!

"All in all I reckon I did over a million dollars on drugs . . . *cash*. Plus, I wasted another million on foolish deeds and doings . . . like, someone would want to borrow money and I'd GIVE them $10,000. And then there was an old girlfriend's father who swore on a coupla gas mines, so I wrote him a cheque for $30,000 and never saw him again. Man, was I stupid!

"But a good time for me was going down to this park in Florida, or over to Sheep's Meadow in New York, and tripping like a zombie. One lady I used to know would have a big water pistol full of LSD, and she'd squirt you in the face and you'd be tripping for days! I mean, I'd go to parties and it'd be like 'OK, find your corner' y'know, somewhere where you could drop when you'd had enough drugs. I'd pass out all the time and when I'd wake up they'd go, 'Hey man you just had a seizure, you'd better take it easy . . .' And I'd go, 'Fuck that man, gimme the pipe,' and I'd put another rock of something in it and WHOOPDEEDOO! I'd be

away again. I thought I was the coolest dude in town, 'cos I'd do everything to the limit. I was too screwed up to see just what an asshole I really was.

"But I don't wanna tell kids 'Don't do drugs', because when I was young I did what everybody told me *not* to. However, I wouldn't mind doing a video for kids showing me having an epileptic fit with a needle in my arm, or puking up blood after a show. That's the reality of drugs, and I think it'd be much more effective than a parent saying *'Don't* . . .'

"I sometimes think it'd be good for kids to take drugs so they feel how great it is to come clean. That's real sick I know, but I think that sometimes. The thing is, any drug addict or alcoholic who comes clean just becomes an even more warm-hearted, wonderful person, because they know what it's like to become human again, and they think very positively. And if you have positive thinking in your life you can become a rock 'n' roll star, the President of the United States, a rhino artificial inseminator . . . anything!

"So now I can go to Jim Vallance's house on a Friday and come home on a Sunday with a cassette of three new songs in my pocket. A coupla years ago I would've gone over with an ounce of cocaine and come home on Sunday not even knowing whose house I'd been to!

"Man, I'm a superstar and that's a great thing to think about, but my heart is only flesh and blood and it can only take so much, no matter who I am. Doing drugs is like ejaculating, but God only lets you orgasm for a few seconds, and there's a reason for that. If people could hit a button and have an orgasm they'd be doing it non-stop. But the human body isn't made that way, so you have to be extra careful with it.

"I don't wanna die right now – not today – so I figure I won't take any drugs today. I can't say I won't wake up in the morning and smoke a bowlful of hash, because I'm an addict and addicts don't fully recover just like that. But today I'll settle for a glass of water and a peach and at least I *will* wake up tomorrow!

"I feel like I'm a walking miracle . . . like there's a light glowing around me. I feel so good now it's unbelievable. I haven't touched any drug for a year and I'm walking around about a foot off the ground. It's like when you get myopia and you get your first glasses . . . suddenly you can see, everything comes into focus!"

Aerosmith had certainly come into focus as far as British rock fans were concerned, and 'Permanent Vacation' vaulted off the back of an endless stream of rave reviews straight into the UK album charts . . .

"Everybody's flipped over 'Permanent Vacation'," said Tyler, "and the reason why it's so

The many colours
and costumes of
Steven Tyler.

much better than the last album is that we did it straight. With the last one we'd come up with a guitar riff and then we'd be off in the bathroom snorting like assholes. But this time we gave it 101 per cent and it shows.''

Back home in the States the record had outsold 'Done With Mirrors' in two weeks according to Tyler, and such was the upsurgence in popularity and demand for Aerosmith in America that a British tour planned for August had to be pulled at the last minute to enable the band to capitalise on their domestic success, leaving those British fans who'd actually purchased tickets to the shows seething with indignation.

The US tour actually kicked off in Binghamton, New York, on October 16. As usual the band had rehearsed at the opening venue for a few days prior to that first show, but this time rehearsals were strict, hard-working affairs with everyone going through their paces in earnest, instead of half-hearted attempts to get everyone on one stage at the same time.

After working around New York State outposts like Buffalo and Syracuse, the 'Permanent Vacation' tour slipped into Canada for dates in Toronto and Montreal, and then worked its way down the East Coast throughout November, typically doing two shows on consecutive days and then having a day off.

"I'm having so much fun," Tyler enthused at the time. "Getting up in the afternoon, flying to a show, rocking the ass off 20,000 maniacs, flying home at midnight and sitting up till three in the morning just thinking about how beautiful life is.''

All the same, Christmas 1987 came as a welcome break for the band – a strangely sober experience that was spent with families, a traditional gesture of cosy homeliness new to raving gypsies like Aerosmith. Perry was now married to his second wife Billie, and between them they had three kids – Adrian from Joe's first marriage, Aaron from Billie's and Anthony from their own relationship. Brad and Karen Whitford (Brad having split from Laurie years before) now had Zachary as an addition to their family, and Joey and April Kramer were the parents of son Jesse Sky and daughter Asia, from April's first marriage. Tom and Terry Hamilton, meanwhile, were still together after "a lifetime" of unwavering wedlock, although they hadn't yet started a family, and Steven Tyler was still with longstanding girlfriend Teresa Barrick, the designer of many of his outrageous stage costumes, whom he was to marry in Tulsa, Oklahoma, on May 28, 1988.

By the middle of January, however, duty called again for the band, and the second leg of the mammoth trek got underway in Seattle, Washington, rumbling through California during late January/early February, taking in Texas, Nevada, Arizona, Oklahoma and Louisiana during the rest of February, and then criss-crossing the States and Canada almost non-stop right up until

"The Aerosmith tour was the first rock 'n' roll tour we've done . . . the vibe between us and them was great. Those guys are just amazing."

SLASH, GUNS N' ROSES

May 22 in Albuquerque, New Mexico, when a well-earned breather was granted.

June was vacation time for Aerosmith, but this time it wouldn't be permanent, and by July 17 the band were back on the road again in Hoffman Estates, Illinois, for a third leg of touring which would stretch well into September. In total the band had spent almost 10 months on the road during that past year, playing something like 130 shows in all. It was a feat of stamina, endurance and intense application that they couldn't possibly have achieved in their previous state of dementia, but it was hard work eradicating temptation from the daily lives of those whose natural working environment was riddled with booze and drugs.

To that end precautions were taken by manager Tim Collins (now parted from Steve Barrisso) to keep his band on the straight and narrow. At hotels the personal mini-bars installed in each room were emptied before any band member set foot through the door, road crew and other backstage personnel were banned from drinking alcohol in front of the band and, most imperative of all, instructions to the effect that drink and drugs

must be kept away from the band at all times were passed on to all support acts – Dokken on the first leg, White Lion on the second leg . . . and particularly Guns n' Roses, who joined the jaunt on its last lap.

The very fact that Guns n' Roses opened for Aerosmith on part of the 'Permanent Vacation' tour was indicative of the pulling power that the band now commanded. Guns n' Roses themselves were well on the way to becoming as big an attraction as their peers, with the 'Appetite For Destruction' album, released in August 1987, swiftly heading towards the multi-platinum status it eventually reached when the Roses exploded worldwide in 1988.

The bill was undoubtedly one of the strongest to hit the road in years, and one show at the 63,000 capacity Giants Stadium in New Jersey on August 16 was particularly memorable, as it also featured Deep Purple sandwiched between the two. That the mighty Deep Purple would be made to support another band was pretty unthinkable at the time, but it was the Aerosmith/Guns coupling which was the most intriguing, a contest made even more fascinating by the fact that many observers saw Guns n' Roses as Sons Of Aerosmith, in much the same way as Aerosmith were cited as direct descendants of The Stones a generation before. To compound the comparison still further, it was clear the young LA band were going through the same toxic troubles that the 'Smiths had encountered in *their* youth.

"They're so much like we used to be, it's uncanny," Tyler told the author during the latter half of the tour. "I mean, their bass player (Duff McKagen) *is* Tom Hamilton – tall, blond, same demeanour! Slash *is* Joe Perry – dark hair, moody, same demeanour! Izzy *is* Brad. And Steven Adler is *very* similar to Joey Kramer. I mean, sometimes I walk into the dressing room with those guys and it's like I'm with my own band!

"And then there's Axl – he's just the kind of 'trash-the-dressing-room' ego-maniac that I used to be.

"But I never talk down to the guys in Guns n' Roses. I mean, I'm always there if they want to talk about it – I can tell them exactly how screwed up I was, and what I did with it – but I don't wanna get into the 'preaching trip'."

Tyler admitted that it was "a bitch to stay straight – not because I've been around the guys in Guns n' Roses, but because all the kids are getting drunk, smoking pot and getting high at our shows." But it was clear he was enjoying the 'fatherly' role he'd assumed with his young support act, so much so that those who worked on tour claim the singer almost 'adopted' Axl Rose as his son!

For their part, Guns n' Roses could hardly believe they were on the same bill as their boyhood idols, and even in their often drug-deranged state faithfully adhered to the restrictions that were imposed on them by Aerosmith's management. They didn't always manage to stay out of trouble when the calming influence of their heroes wasn't around though: in Philadelphia Axl had a punch-up with a parking lot attendant that landed him in a police cell half an hour before show-time, and the tetchy singer also saw fit to throw a coffee table through a hotel window elsewhere on the tour. The wise old pros in Aerosmith, meanwhile, just smirked knowingly.

Good-natured craziness did prevail right until the end of the tour though. On the second from last night in California, G n' R drummer Steven Adler zipped across the stage on a motorised skateboard during 'Dude (Looks Like A Lady)'. In retaliation, various Aerosmith roadies donned gorilla costumes the following night to hop around the stage during G n' R's 'Welcome To The Jungle', while a Tarzan-lookalike swung from a vine.

After the jungle japes Axl joked to the audience, "Just remember, they have to play next . . ." but what actually happened during Aerosmith's set was one legendary jam on 'Mama Kin', with the two singers howling into an impromptu duet, and Duff and Slash jamming next to Tom, Brad and Joe.

Indeed, camaraderie between the two bands had been so strong that Steven and Joe's wives had specially-printed tour T-shirts featuring all the rehab centres on the back instead of concert venues made up and given to Guns n' Roses. And to cap it all, backstage after the last show of the tour Aerosmith presented their support act and

their management with a set of ultra-expensive Halliburton luggage each, as well as personalised Aerosmith/Guns n' Roses tour jackets.

To say the tour was an unmitigated success would be an understatement of 'Hitler was a naughty boy' proportions. The whole bandwagon had snowballed into record-breaking feats: the album had reached number 11 on the US Billboard chart, going on to sell over four million copies over the next two years, and the singles 'Dude . . .', 'Angel' and 'Rag Doll' had hit 14, 3 and 17 respectively. In Britain, 'Permanent Vacation' had peaked at 37 on the album charts (thereby notching up the band's first hit album in the UK), with 'Dude . . .' getting to 45 in October 1987 and 'Angel' squeezing in at 69 during April 1988 on the singles chart.

And there was more to come: three videos were also released during the 'Permanent Vacation' campaign to quench the raging thirst of desperate Aerosmith fans (and bag a few extra coppers). *Video Scrapbook* was just that, an hour-long delve into the band's own private collection of concert footage and off-stage tomfoolery. *3 × 5* was a package containing the three Marty Callner videos for 'Dude . . .', 'Angel' and 'Rag Doll'. And *Live Texxas Jam* was a flashback to the Dallas Cotton Bowl extravaganza in July 1978, released the same month (October 1988) as Columbia rustled up another 'greatest hits' compilation album called 'Gems', in typical old-record-company-cashes-in style.

It seemed as though everyone was trying to take a slice of Aerosmith now that the goose that laid the golden egg was churning them out battery-hen fashion. But for those who'd witnessed the band's dramatic and disgusting fall from grace a few years earlier, the spectacle of Aerosmith flying high again was indeed a sight for sore eyes.

Far left: Aerosmith proteges Guns n' Roses.
Left: Tyler outside his New York apartment.
Below: Perry with new wife Billie and (below) Tyler, Hamilton and Whitford with various members of Bon Jovi.

CHAPTER TEN

PUMP UP THE VOLUME!

"OH SHIT, WHAT ARE WE gonna do now?''

When the 'Permanent Vacation' carousel finally ground to a halt in September 1988 and the five exhausted Aeromen staggered onto *terra firma* for the first time in over a year, momentum dictated there was barely time to draw breath before the band were back in pre-production for another album.

There was already a neat little stockpile of ideas that the band had built over the months – tentative titles like 'Is Anybody Out There' and 'Worlds Collide', and even a possible LP name in 'Bobbing For Piranhas' according to a tongue-in-cheek Tyler.

But the extent of the task before them – following such a mega-successful album as 'Permanent Vacation' – hit home hard when their world had stopped spinning, and Tyler later confessed to being daunted by the prospect.

Still, here were the 'elder statesmen' of rock, now wise old owls capable of anything, with the key of life pushed well down in their pockets. Along with fellow stalwarts Ozzy Osbourne and Lemmy from Motorhead they'd even been portrayed in Penelope Spheeris' rock documentary film *The Decline Of Western Civilisation Part II: The Metal Years* (sort of *Spinal Tap* for real) as level-headed saviours amongst an idiotic new wave of over-the-top heavy metal kids bent on self-destruction. The irony wasn't lost on any of Tyler's troupers.

And so it was with two months of rehearsals and writing sessions behind them that Aerosmith reconvened in Vancouver during January of 1989 to begin recording their new album with producer Bruce Fairbairn. The picture now was of serious musicians going to work rather than wild party animals piling into a studio to get drunk for a month, and in their new 'parental' role in rock they even took under their wing the hell-raising Motley Crue, who were also at Little Mountain Studios recording their 'Dr Feelgood' album.

''We'd all grown up with Aerosmith,'' Crue bassist Nikki Sixx confided to the author, ''but we knew of their 'problems'. At the listening party for our 'Shout At The Devil' album in the Kit Kat Club

(an LA strip joint) someone told me Joe Perry had showed up. We were thrilled to death, but when I went to look for him I found him passed out in the corner. It was pretty sad.

"But we fell into the same rock 'n' roll trap. The next time I met Aerosmith was after one of their 'Permanent Vacation' shows at The Forum in LA. Six days earlier I'd had a heroin overdose and I'd only just recovered . . . so I'm walking backstage feeling very nervous about meeting my heroes when Steven Tyler comes over and shouts at me, 'Hey man, whaddya think ya doin'?! Are you crazy? What's wrong with you?' He really ripped into me. So we talked and talked and our friendship sort of grew out of our AA (Alcoholics Anonymous) connections – y'know, this common ground of trying to stay alive. I even asked Steven if he'd be my sponsor and he agreed, but what with both our touring commitments we never really got that together.

"So when we got to Vancouver and found Aerosmith were recording their album next door to us we were completely blown away. There was one lobby between the studios and we'd all hang out there, watching TV, exchanging stories, going out to strip joints . . ."

miles into the run when it started to pour with rain. So we were running around this lake talking about rock 'n' roll and how we were all gonna kick some ass next year an' stuff . . . and we're all drenched! We were laughing our butts off, it was an experience I'll still be thinking about when I'm an old guy in my rocking chair!''

Back in the studio the 'old guys' in Aerosmith were rocking up something of a storm too. After commenting in the press that they felt parts of 'Permanent Vacation' were a little too commercial (''I was scared to death to use a couple of the tracks on that record, I thought the kids would flip out because it just wasn't Aerosmith,'' said Tyler, with 'Angel' – ironically their biggest *ever* hit single – foremost in mind), the emphasis this time was on producing something a little harder, more exotic and creating ''a certain mystique'' as Tyler put it. Influences as bizarre as Zydeco and Cajun music had even filtered through to the band, and in Vancouver they'd been introduced to a collector of ethnic instruments from all over the world, who helped them create many of the weird sounds they were striving for.

''This guy (Randy Raine Reusch) had a room with hundreds, maybe thousands of them,'' said Tyler. ''Little bamboo things, big bamboo things, stuff made from human femurs. He just brought everything that we picked out down to the studio and let us jam with them, and what we came up with we used as interludes to tie the whole album together.''

The particularly odd intro to one track, 'Voodoo Medicine Man', came from a closer-to-home source though. During the Guns n' Roses tour Tyler became interested in some of the strange tapes rhythm guitarist Izzy Stradlin had collected, and managed to acquire a couple which included African rituals and witchcraft. These Tyler fused with a few other curiosities he'd hoarded years before, and the result seemed to tickle the tastebuds of the singer.

''Then Joe got this water-phone thing from a guy called Richard Waters,'' he enthused. ''It's like a metal vase with rods sticking out and you fill it with water and swill them around a bit and you play it with a violin bow. That's the sound we used at the beginning of 'Janie's Got A Gun'.''

The commercial angle of the record wasn't entirely overlooked, however. Geffen was determined that the formula which had proved so successful with 'Permanent Vacation' should be repeated while the going was good, and Desmond Child and Jim Vallance were duly wheeled in to add their radio-friendly magic. As ever the Tyler/

Tyler also agreed to sing some backing vocals on the Crue's album, and the two bands even found themselves pumping iron together, instead of popping pills.

''We were all staying at the same hotel,'' says Nikki, ''and there was a gym in the basement where we'd all work out. There'd be some guys from The Cult, us, some of the Aerosmith guys . . . all these supposedly screwed up rock stars pumping weights in the same room!

''One time we went for a run about 10 o'clock in the morning – me, Tom Hamilton, Steven Tyler and a coupla other guys – and we'd got about two

"Aerosmith are one of the greatest live acts of all time, on a par with The Rolling Stones and Dogs D'Amour!"

BAM BAM, DOGS D'AMOUR

Perry team was responsible for most of the original material, but Child put his stamp on the likes of 'F.I.N.E.' and 'What It Takes', while Vallance poked his nose into 'The Other Side' and 'Young Lust'.

'Young Lust' actually got the whole record rolling, cracking a furious pace with the usual hot-lipped hotch-potch of high-kicking licks and low-level laughs ('You better keep your daughter inside/Or she's gonna get a dose of my pride'). It was the most startling album opener since 'Toys In The Attic', tumbling directly into 'F.I.N.E.' in much the same way as 'Rats In The Cellar' would cave into 'I Wanna Know Why' at the start of many Aero shows in the late seventies; the killer combination was a good example of just why Aerosmith are now virtually untouchable in the hard rock league.

'F.I.N.E.' itself was one big adrenalin-rush, heart-stopping Aerosmith in the classic raunch 'n' roll mode – like The Stones with a thousand volts up their trouser legs. With a typical Tyler twist the letters stood for something quite different from their superficial meaning (''Fucked-up, Insecure, Neurotic and Emotional,'' explained the singer later, ''exactly what I was for many years!''), and lyrically the sleaze was dripping from the walls again, too. 'I shove my tongue right between your cheeks/I haven't made love now for 25/I heard you're so tight you're loving squeaks/But I'm ready, so ready . . .'

The saucy humour continued with 'Love In An Elevator', complete with its silly, sexy intro, a track Perry later confessed was inspired by several Holiday Inn encounters with inevitable results. But the new-found maturity in the band's writing had inspired more than just clever innuendo, and while 'Monkey On My Back' dealt with Tyler's drug addiction, 'Janie's Got A Gun' tackled the terrifying topic of child abuse and focused on the true story of a girl who shot her own father in retaliation. It was perhaps the most pointed and poignant

Aerosmith song to date.

The good times rolled again on side two though: 'The Other Side' marked the return of The Margarita Horns as it breezed through a bouncing, brass-backed boogie with strong Beatles overtones (particularly on the backing vocals), 'My Girl' rattled brazenly like the kid brother of 'Young Lust' and 'Don't Get Mad, Get Even' bristled with a bluesy, boozy 12-bar vengeance.

Next was 'Voodoo Medicine Man', a mysterious meander through witchcraft and things that go bump in the jungle, and finally 'What It Takes' summoned up all its lump-in-the-throat emotion to round the whole thing off in rousing ballad style. A strange move when you consider the band's contempt for 'Angel', the song's direct counterpart on 'Permanent Vacation'.

Overall though, the new 'Smith album was better than '. . . Vacation' – slightly harder, more cohesive and more recognisably Aerosmith. Its title, after months of agonising, was finally revealed as 'Pump', a word which Brad Whitford related to the pumping of a heart, but which the album's artwork (two mounted trucks) suggested had more of a sexual connotation (naturally!). And although it initially received some opposition from Tyler, the title was certainly more imaginative than another of the suggestions being considered: 'Aerosmith'.

Below: Tyler receives an award for 'Pump' in Kensington, West London, August 1990.

PUMP UP THE VOLUME!

'Pump' was unveiled to an anxious public on September 12, shipping platinum and instantly hailed a modern masterpiece almost as par for the course. Five-star reviews rained in from the rock press worldwide, and what with the band's appeal now stretching to a *Top Of The Pops* audience and beyond, the more mainstream music media found themselves paying lip-service to the band as well.

'Love In An Elevator', the first single accompanied by another sniggersome Marty Callner video, had already been a hit in August, crashing into the charts at number five in America and 13 in the UK, while the album peaked at number five in the US and three in Britain. In November 'Janie's Got A Gun' became the second hit from the album, reaching number four in the States and also charting in the UK, and by the summer of 1990 both 'What It Takes' and 'The Other Side' had gatecrashed the US charts – the former getting to number nine, the latter reaching 22 – whereas in Britain a re-released 'Dude . . .' got to number 20 and 'The Other Side' made 46.

During the August of 1989 Tyler and Perry made another promotional trip to Europe, this time bearing good tidings of a full Euro-tour in the Autumn instead of excuses for cancellations, and by October 18 the band were ready to kick off the 'Pump' world tour with a date at the 8000-seater Cologne Sporthalle in Germany – their first show on European soil for just over 12 years. Italy was next – two shows in Florence and Milan – and then came one-offs in France at Le Zenith, Paris, Belgium at Forêt Nationale, Brussels, and the Netherlands at Rijnhal, Arnhem, before an eight-date jaunt in Germany saw them performing to a total of 59,000 people in 11 days.

Scandinavia also had the privilege of seeing Aerosmith this time around, with the band stopping off in Copenhagen, Denmark, on October 10 and Stockholm, Sweden, the following day before taking two days off and then marching into London like conquering heroes. Anticipation of their arrival had built to a fever pitch by this time, and tickets for any show on the British tour were harder to come by than a pools win. Fewer rock tours had ever been more eagerly awaited than this one.

Above: Joe Perry and Steven Tyler with comedian Sam Kinnisan (extreme right) at Aerosmith's induction to 'Rock Walk', March 1990. Above right: Aerosmith win . . . hands down!

And so it was at the Hammersmith Odeon in London on Tuesday November 14 that Aerosmith finally let a new generation of British rock fans know what all the fuss was about. The place was packed, the excitement was electric and EVERYONE was there to see ultimate proof that Tyler was fitter than the entire Soviet Olympic gymnastics team, that Joe Perry had more killer riffs than any of his contemporaries and that the band *left out* more classics from their set than most bands ever record.

The following night even Whitesnake's David Coverdale was there to amble on-stage for an encore version of The Beatles' 'I'm Down'.

Coverdale was also one of the guests at the band's after-show party at the Bombay Brasserie in Knightsbridge, along with the rest of London's desperate ligging fraternity, who'd managed to beg, blag or bully their way into the bash.

With one day to recover from an excess of Perrier and peanuts at the party, the band completed their third London show at Wembley Arena on October 17, and then set off around the country for two shows at Birmingham's 11,500 capacity NEC, one at the City Hall in Newcastle, one at The Forum in Livingstone in Scotland and one at the Antrim Forum in Belfast before a final visit to Wembley wrapped up the tour. It had been

an unqualified success, the talking point of the year as far as British rock fans were concerned, a fact reflected by the readers' polls in all the Brit rock comix. In *RAW* magazine the 'Smiths won several categories: Best Album ('Pump'), Best Single ('Love In An Elevator') and Best Promo Video (ditto). In *Kerrang!* they waltzed away as Best Band, with 'Pump' being Best Album, Tyler being Best Male Singer, and the UK foray being voted Best Tour.

* * *

Back in the States, Aerosmith shaped up for the first US leg of the tour by announcing new sensations Skid Row as support act. On the UK tour they'd shared dates with a cluster of up 'n' coming Brit acts such as The Quireboys, Thunder, Balaam And The Angel and Little Angels, giving each band a fair crack of the whip. And the policy of taking on the hottest young talent around, which had begun with the Guns n' Roses tour in 1988, was continued with the choice of the in-vogue Skids. Here was a band untouched by

"Aerosmith? Ain't those the guys influenced by Guns n' Roses!?"

DAVE MUSTAINE, MEGADETH

Left: Aerosmith at Les Paul's 75th birthday party, Hard Rock Cafe, New York, summer 1990. Above right: Tyler with ex-Hanoi Rocker Mike Monroe. Middle right: Perry and Tyler at yet another award ceremony. Below right: Tyler gets to the point with Ratt vocalist Stephen Pearcey.

complacency, ready to slug it out in public with any precocious upstarts who fancied their chances. Few bands of Aerosmith's age would've taken the potential risk of being given a good run for their money by the support act.

The tour began on December 15 at the Civic Center in Charlestown, West Virginia, and weaved its way across Virginia and Maryland when a Christmas break brought a temporary halt to proceedings. The day after Boxing Day the trucks were rolling again though, and the band saw in the New Year in their hometown with three nights at the 14,000-capacity Boston Garden.

Canada was next, a trip which included a show at the awesome 26,500-seater Skydome in Toronto, and then it was box office bonanzas all the way from New York's Nassau Coliseum (21,086) to New Jersey (Meadowlands – 21,170), and from Phoenix (Campion Terrace – 21,666) to Tacoma (Tacoma Dome – 21,770). Elsewhere there were two nights at the 17,000-seater Spectrum in Philadelphia, three nights at the 15,000-seater Great Western Forum in Inglewood, California, and two consecutive nights at the 16,000-capacity Cow Palace in San Francisco.

The tour quickly inked itself into the annals of rock history as one to match the Guns n' Roses

extravaganza, and with the exception of one unsavoury incident at the Springfield Civic Center in Massachusetts on December 27, when singer Sebastian Bach caused a storm by jumping into the crowd to attack someone who'd hit him with a bottle during the set (an incident which ended up with Bach being arrested and charged for assault, assault and battery and 'mayhem'), the experience was a happy one for both parties.

"The idea of playing on the same stage as Aerosmith is one that constantly blows my mind," said guitarist Dave Sabo. "It's a dream come true for anyone who grew up on American rock in the seventies."

For their part the Skids respected the stipulations which Aerosmith now laid down for support bands. Alcohol was confined to their dressing room, and had to be carried in paper cups if anyone wanted to wander around the venue with it.

"We do our fair share of partying," bassist Rachel Bolan explained, "but we never overstep our boundaries."

Meanwhile, Aerosmith had established a whole different approach to touring, which contrasted sharply with the hell-raising escapades of yore.

"In the old days," laughed Tyler, "Joe had all the names of the groupies and dealers on a computer disc. Now we just have tour books telling us how many treadmills the hotel gym has."

It was all a bit clouded in fantasy, a little too far-

SEVENTY FOUR

fetched for some to grasp. But it was true all right, and the accolades didn't stop. On March 6 it was even a case of Five Go To Hollywood, where the band were inducted into Hollywood's Rock Walk, leaving handprints and signatures in a slab of wet concrete just as legends like Chuck Berry, Bo Diddley, Jerry Lee Lewis and Stevie Wonder had done before them. It was true all right – the proof was in the pavement!

The Skid Row liaison finally ended on Saturday, March 31, at the Salt Palace in Salt Lake City, with a few of the more mischievous souls in the Aerosmith crew marking the occasion by dropping a banner behind the openers during their set which read: 'THE SKIDS SLEEP WITH MILLI VANILLI', a stinging insult. Moments later the band's management appeared on-stage as pizza-

delivery boys in full mad-chef regalia, and proceedings deteriorated from there.

After a short break Aerosmith were back on the road in Jacksonville, Florida, on April 17, honouring an increasing number of commitments and toiling through a schedule so tight that manager Tim Collins refused to allow anyone from the Aerosmith camp to co-operate on the research for this book, on the basis that the band had the next six months of their lives mapped out down to the last minute – literally! – and therefore couldn't *possibly* spare even five minutes on the phone.

Still, the band were bearing up to the strain and managing to stay straight and sober along the way. Getting high this time around meant nothing more than flying between shows in Ferdinand Marcos' former jet, the Cessna Citation 2 which the 'Smiths had christened 'Aeroforce 1'. And while renting the plane wasn't cheap, with sales figures for 'Pump' passing the four million mark comfortably, they could afford such luxuries once again.

April and May saw the band devour dates across the southern states and up the East Coast to Ohio and Michigan, The Black Crowes, another hot new noise on the rock block, then taking over the most prestigious of support slots. June found Aerosmith picking up several accolades at the International Rock Awards ceremony in New York – winning an Elvis statuette for being voted 'Artist Of The Year', with Tyler voted winner of the MVP (Most Valuable Player) category – and also performing as specially invited guests at guitar legend Les Paul's 75th birthday bash at New York's Hard Rock Café. Fittingly, the month culminated in two huge shows, the 62,000-capacity Canadian National Exhibition Center in Toronto (with Metallica and Warrant joining The Black Crowes on the bill), and the 30,000-seater Silver Stadium in Rochester, New York.

The fourth US leg of the 'Pump' world tour eventually climaxed at the Capitol Center in Landover, Maryland, on July 28, with Aerosmith having played to a total of one-and-three-quarter million fans in America since the first leg back in December, an average of 15,000 punters per night over 115 nights. The tour had been an incredible achievement, commercially, physically and mentally for a band who many thought had peaked 12 years before, and a tremendous advertisement for the new health-conscious age of fitness, non-fatty foods and fizzy water!

By the time Aerosmith arrived at the Point Theatre in Dublin on August 15 for a show with The Quireboys designed as a warm-up for their 'Special Guest' slot on the Monsters Of Rock tour during August and September, they'd established themselves as the second highest grossing live act in the US, having sold some $25 million worth of tickets in the first half of 1990 alone.

The one and only act ahead of Aerosmith? The Rolling Stones, of course . . .

SWEET EMOTION (REVISITED)

IT'S MONDAY, AUGUST 20, 1990, two days after the Donington festival, and the streets of Soho in London are buzzing with people in Aerosmith T-shirts. The band's 'secret' gig at the infamous Marquee Club had been the worst-kept secret of the year in rock circles, and tonight the entire British rock industry seem to be crammed into the club's modest confines, shoulder-to-shoulder with the very few punters lucky enough to have bought a ticket during the 50 minutes or so that they were on sale.

Just before nine o'clock the dressing room door behind Joey Kramer's drum kit opens and Steven Tyler leads the way to the stage with the just-seen-a-ghost screams of 850 normally well-balanced citizens ringing around the place. Then, with no further ado, it's 'Monkey On My Back', 'F.I.N.E.', 'Walking The Dog', 'Janie's Got A Gun', 'Back In The Saddle', 'One Way Street', 'Big Ten Inch Record', 'Mama Kin', 'Voodoo Medicine Man', 'What It Takes', 'Milk Cow Blues' and 'Toys In The Attic', leaving the audience – including members of The Dan Reed Network, The Quireboys, Thunder, Queensryche, Ratt, Little Angels and Iron Maiden – almost too exhausted to gasp in amazement as Jimmy Page saunters on-stage for the second time in 48 hours to join Aerosmith, this time for a six-song encore.

With Page and Perry swopping licks toe-to-toe and Tyler dancing around what space there is left on the postage stamp stage, the band rolls through a significant selection of songs, from 'Ain't Got You' and The Yardbirds' 'Think About It', to Hendrix's 'Red House', Led Zeppelin's 'Immigrant Song' and finally the old chestnut, 'Train Kept A Rollin'' – songs which acted as catalysts for the fledgling outfit all those years ago. The atmosphere is pure party stuff, like a hundred New Year's Eves in one, and not even the ill-timed backline failure just as Page was about to take a solo in 'Red House' could spit on the fireworks.

As a parting shot Aerosmith return one last time with a fearsome foursome – 'Young Lust', 'Dream On', 'Love In An Elevator' and 'Walk This Way' – and then it's over, a musical exclamation mark burnt into the memory of 850 people forever.

Opposite left: Tyler
at the MTV Awards,
1990.
Below: The
legendary Marquee
gig with special
guest Jimmy Page,
August 1990.

The Show Of The Century? The best gig
EVER? Superlatives were bandied about in the
wake of the Marquee knees-up with a wild
abandon which brought into question the sanity of
many. But amid the furore, the glory of that hot
August night was impossible to deny. At the post-
show party in Le Meridian Hotel near Piccadilly
Circus, even Tyler had to concede it was ''a pretty
good evening's work.''

For Aerosmith there were a few more ''pretty
good evenings'' ahead of them in their 20th
anniversary year, not least a date at the MTV
Awards ceremony in LA on September 6, which
yielded awards for Best Heavy Metal Video ('Love
In An Elevator') and Viewers' Choice. It seemed
there was no limit to the popularity of Uncle Sam's
favourite nephews.

Oh yeah . . . and then there was that little matter
of a world tour to complete, with appointments in
Japan and Australia (for the first time) whisking
them through to October, when the stadia of their
homeland beckoned once more. The road
stretched beyond the horizon. Another day,
another few thousand dollars . . .

Who said it was only rock 'n' roll?

"They're a great band. Steven Tyler? Mr Energy! I'd like to be as fit as him when I get to his age! Ha!"

JIMMY PAGE

SINGLES (7-INCH)

Dream On/Somebody
CBS 1898 November 1973

Dream On/Somebody
CBS 4000 April 1976 (reissue)

Last Child/Combination
CBS 4452 August 1976

Walk This Way/Uncle Salty
CBS 6584 February 1977

Remember (Walking In The Sand)/Bone To Bone
CBS 8220 February 1980

Walk This Way/Instrumental (With Run DMC)
London LON 104 August 1986

Dude (Looks Like A Lady)/Simoriah
Geffen GEF 29 October 1987

Angel/Girl Keeps Coming Apart
Geffen GEF 34 April 1988

Love In An Elevator/Young Lust
Geffen GEF 63 August 1989 (Also issued with free patch, on GEF 63X)

Janie's Got A Gun/Voodoo Medicine Man
Geffen GEF 68 November 1989

Dude (Looks Like A Lady)/Monkey On My Back
Geffen GEF 72 February 1990 (Also issued as picture disc, on GEF 72P)

Rag Doll/Simoriah
Geffen GEF 76 June 1990

The Other Side/My Girl
Geffen GEF 79 October 1990

SINGLES (12-INCH)

Walk This Way/Instrumental/My Adidas (With Run DMC)
London LONX 104 August 1986

Dude (Looks Like A Lady)/Simoriah/Once Is Enough
Geffen GEF 29T October 1987 (Also issued as picture disc, on GEF 29TP)

Angel/Girl Keeps Coming Apart
Geffen GEF 34T April 1988 (Also issued as picture disc, on GEF 34TP)

Love In An Elevator/Young Lust/Ain't Enough
Geffen GEF 63T August 1989 (Also issued as picture disc, on GEF 63TP; and with free patch, on GEF 63TX)

Janie's Got A Gun/Voodoo Medicine Man
Geffen GEF 68T November 1989

Dude (Looks Like A Lady)/Love In An Elevator (live)/Walk This Way (live)
Geffen GEF 72T February 1990 (Also issued with free patch, on GEF 72TW)

Rag Doll (Version 1)/Mama Kin (live)/Dream On (live)
Geffen GEF 76T June 1990 (Also issued with free patch, on GEF 76TW)

The Other Side/Theme From Wayne's World/The Other Side/My Girl
Geffen GEF 79T October 1990

The Other Side/Love In An Elevator/Dude (Looks Like A Lady)/Walk This Way
Geffen GEF 79TG October 1990 (gatefold sleeve)

CASSETTE SINGLES

Dude (Looks Like A Lady)/Simoriah
Geffen GEF 29C October 1987

Angel/Girl Keeps Coming Apart
Geffen GEF 34C April 1988

Love In An Elevator/Young Lust
Geffen GEF 63C August 1989

Janie's Got A Gun/Voodoo Medicine Man
Geffen GEF 68C November 1989

Dude (Looks Like A Lady)/Monkey On My Back
Geffen GEF 72C February 1990

Rag Doll/Simoriah
Geffen GEF 76C June 1990

The Other Side/My Girl
Geffen GEF 79C October 1990

CD SINGLES

Angel/Angel (remix)/Girl Keeps Coming Apart/Dude (Looks Like A Lady)
Geffen GEF 34CD April 1988

Love In An Elevator/Young Lust/Ain't Enough
Geffen GEF 63CD August 1989

Janie's Got A Gun/Voodoo Medicine Man
Geffen GEF 68CD November 1989

Dude (Looks Like A Lady)/Love In An Elevator (live)/Walk This Way (live)
Geffen GEF 72CD February 1990

Rag Doll (version 1)/Mama Kin (live)/Dream On (live)
Geffen GEF 76CD June 1990

The Other Side/Theme From Wayne's World/The Other Side/My Girl
Geffen GEF 79CD October 1990

ALBUMS

AEROSMITH
Side 1: Make It/Somebody/Dream On/One Way Street
Side 2: Mama Kin/Write Me/Movin' Out/Walkin' The Dog
CBS 65486 September 1974

GET YOUR WINGS
Side 1: Same Old Song And Dance/Lord Of The Thighs/Spaced/Woman Of The World
Side 2: SOS (Too Bad)/Train Kept A Rollin'/Seasons Of Wither/Pandora's Box
CBS 80015 November 1974

TOYS IN THE ATTIC
Side 1: Toys In The Attic/Uncle Salty/Adam's Apple/Walk This Way/Big Ten Inch Record
Side 2: Sweet Emotion/No More No More/Round And Round/You See Me Crying
CBS 80773 July 1975

ROCKS
Side 1: Back In The Saddle/Last Child/Rats In The Cellar/Combination
Side 2: Sick As A Dog/Nobody's Fault/Get The Lead Out/Lick And A Promise/Home Tonight
CBS 81397 June 1976

BOOTLEG

DRAW THE LINE
Side 1: Draw The Line/I Wanna Know Why/Critical Mass/Get
It Up/Bright Light Fright
Side 2: Kings And Queens/The Hand That Feeds/Sight For
Sore Eyes/Milk Cow Blues
CBS 82147 January 1978

SGT. PEPPER'S LONELY HEARTS CLUB BAND
(Double film soundtrack LP featuring 'Come Together')
A&M AMLZ66600 June 1978

LIVE! BOOTLEG
(Double LP)
Side 1: Back In The Saddle/Sweet Emotion/Lord Of The
Thighs/Toys In The Attic
Side 2: Last Child/Come Together/Walk This Way/Sick As A
Dog Side 3: Dream On/Chip Away The Stone/Sight For Sore
Eyes/Mama Kin/SOS (Too Bad)
Side 4: I Ain't Got You/Mother Popcorn/Draw The Line/Train
Kept A Rollin'
CBS 88235 January 1979

NIGHT IN THE RUTS
Side 1: No Surprise/Chiquita/Remember (Walking In The
Sand)/Cheese Cake
Side 2: Three Mile Smile/Reefer Head Woman/Bone To Bone
(Coney Island White Fish Boy)/Think About It/Mia
CBS 83680 January 1980

GREATEST HITS
Side 1: Dream On/Same Old Song And Dance/Sweet
Emotion/Walk This Way/Last'Child
Side 2: Back In The Saddle/Draw The Line/Kings And
Queens/ Come Together/Remember (Walking In The Sand)
CBS 84704 January 1981

ROCK IN A HARD PLACE
Side 1: Jailbait/Lightning Strikes/Bitches Brew/Bolivian
Ragamuffin/Cry Me A River
Side 2: Prelude To Joanie/Joanie's Butterfly/Rock In A Hard
Place (Cheshire Cat)/Jig Is Up/Push Comes To Shove
CBS 85931 October 1982

DONE WITH MIRRORS
Side 1: Let The Music Do The Talking/My Fist Your Face/
Shame On You/The Reason A Dog
Side 2: Sheila/Gypsy Boots/She's On Fire/The Hop
Geffen GEF 26695 December 1985 (Tape includes **'Darkness'**)

CLASSICS LIVE
Side 1: Train Kept A Rollin'/Kings And Queens/Sweet
Emotion/Dream On
Side 2: Mama Kin/Three Mile Smile/Reefer Head Woman/
Lord Of The Thighs/Major Barbra
CBS 26901 September 1986

PERMANENT VACATION
Side 1: Heart's Done Time/Magic Touch/Rag Doll/Simoriah/
Dude (Looks Like A Lady)/St John
Side 2: Hangman Jury/Girl Keeps Coming Apart/Angel/
Permanent Vacation/I'm Down/The Movie
Geffen WX 126 August 1987

GREATEST HITS
CBS 460703–1 February 1988 (reissue)

INTERVIEW PICTURE DISC
Baktabak BAK 2091 April 1988

CLASSICS LIVE VOL II
Side 1: Back In The Saddle/Walk This Way/Movin' Out/Draw
The Line
Side 2: Same Old Song And Dance/Last Child/Let The Music
Do The Talking/Toys In The Attic
CBS 460037–2 November 1988

ANTHOLOGY(Double LP)
Toys In The Attic/Sweet Emotion/Walk This Way (live)/No
More No More/You See Me Crying/Bright Light Fright/Lord
Of The Thighs/Back In The Saddle (live)/Sick As A Dog/
Critical Mass/The Hand That Feeds/Sight For Sore Eyes/
Mother Popcorn/Train Kept A Rollin'/SOS (Too Bad)/Rock In
A Hard Place/Jailbait/Push Comes To Shove/Rats In The
Cellar/Bone To Bone/Dream On
Raw Power RAWLP 037 January 1989

PUMP
Side 1: Young Lust/F.I.N.E./Love In An Elevator/Monkey On
My Back/Janie's Got A Gun
Side 2: The Other Side/My Girl/Don't Get Mad, Get Even/
Voodoo Medicine Man/What It Takes
Geffen WX 304 September 1989

GEMS
Rats In The Cellar/Lick And A Promise/Chip Away The
Stone/No Surprise/Mama Kin/Adam's Apple/Nobody's Fault/
Round And Round/Critical Mass/Lord Of The Thighs/
Jailbait/Train Kept A Rollin'
CBS 463224–2 November 1989

BOOTLEGS
(The publishers point out that the bootlegging of records is
illegal, and that neither they nor the author can entertain any
inquiries as to where or how the following records may be
obtained.)

ALBUMS (Unless otherwise stated)

RATTLESNAKE SHAKE (As 1974)
Side 1: Make It/Somebody/Write Me/Dream On/One Way
Street/Walking The Dog
Side 2: Pandora's Box/Rattlesnake Shake/Train Kept A
Rollin'/Mama Kin
Recorded: Counterpart Studios, New York, 1974.
Cover: Orange/red pic of band and logo.
Quality: Very good stereo.
Comments: Rare live version of Fleetwood Mac's **'Rattlesnake
Shake'**, a forerunner of **'Rats In The Cellar'**; reissued as
'Rattlesnake Shake' LXXXIV No 16, approximately 100
numbered copies.

EROTIC DREAMS (Swingin' Pig Records) 1974
Write Me/Mama Kin/Lord Of The Thighs/Woman Of The
World/Dream On/Pandora's Box/Same Old Song And Dance/
One Way Street/Somebody/Train Kept A Rollin'/Walkin'
The Dog
Recorded: Michigan Palace, Detroit, April 14, 1974.
Cover: Black background with recent colour pic of Tyler and
mike stand.
Quality: Very good.
Comments: European CD bootleg.

LIVE BOOTLEG Vol 2 (Unknown) 1974
Side 1: Write Me/SOS (Too Bad)/Lord Of The Thighs/Dream
On/Same Old Song And Dance
Side 2: Woman Of The World/Train Kept A Rollin'[*]/Walkin'
The Dog/Walk This Way
Recorded: My Father's Place, New York, July 27, 1974, except
[*] recorded at Agora Ballroom, Chicago, March 23, 1978.
Cover: Black and white deluxe.
Quality: Excellent stereo.
Comments: European origin.

AEROSMITH LIVE (Cassette) 1974
Side 1: SOS (Too Bad)/Somebody/Lord Of The Thighs/
Woman Of The World/Dream On
Side 2: Same Old Song And Dance/Walkin' The Dog/Train
Kept A Rollin'
Recorded: Academy Of Music, New York, November 2, 1974.
Quality: Very good.
Comments: Includes ridiculously long drum solo.

LOOK HOMEWARD ANGEL
Side 1: SOS (Too Bad)/Somebody/Dream On/Write Me
Side 2: Walkin' The Dog/Train Kept A Rollin'/Toys In The
Attic
Recorded: New York, 1975.
Cover: Pink tinted pic of band.
Quality: Excellent stereo.
Comments: Reissued on Fantasy Disco F7868 with deluxe
black and white cover; **'Walk This Way'** listed as **'Walkin' The
Dog'** on both covers.

ROCK THIS WAY (TKRWM 1812) 1975
Side 1: SOS (Too Bad)/Somebody/Dream On/Write Me
Side 2: Walk This Way/No More No More/Same Old Song
And Dance/Tots In The Attic
Recorded:New York, 1975.
Cover:Yellow/brown pic of woman's hand holding object with
'Monkey Grip' label on it.
Quality: Excellent stereo.
Comments: Taken from the same concert as **'Look Homeward
Angel'**, with **'No More No More'** and **'Same Old Song And
Dance'** included instead of **'Train Kept A Rollin''**.

STAMP (Unknown) 1976
Side 1: Mama Kin/Write Me/SOS (Too Bad)/Lick And A
Promise/Big Ten Inch Record
Side 2: Sweet Emotion/Rats In The Cellar/Dream On/Lord Of
The Thighs

Recorded: Peoria, Illinois, July 15, 1976
Cover: Stamped.
Quality: Very good mono.
Comments: Rare – only 25 copies pressed.

AEROSMITH LIVE (Cassette) 1976
Side 1: Mama Kin/Write Me/SOS (Too Bad)/Lick And A Promise/Big Ten Inch Record/Sweet Emotion/Rats In The Cellar/Dream On/Lord Of The Thighs
Side 2: Last Child/Walk This Way/Sick As A Dog/Same Old Song And Dance/Train Kept A Rollin'/Get The Lead Out/Milk Cow Blues
Recorded: Madison Square Garden, New York, December 1976.
Quality: Excellent.
Comments: Recorded from sound board.

AEROSMITH LIVE (Cassette) 1976
Side 1: Mama Kin/Write Me/SOS (Too Bad)/Lick And A Promise/Big Ten Inch Record/Sweet Emotion/Rats In The Cellar/Last Child/Lord Of The Thighs
Side 2: Walk This Way/Sick As A Dog/Same Old Song And Dance/Train Kept A Rollin'/Get The Lead Out/Toys In The Attic
Recorded: Boston, December 1976.
Quality: Excellent.
Comments: Recorded the same week as previous bootleg, also from sound board.

SPIRIT OF BOSTON (VM 2637) 1977
Side 1: Mama Kin/SOS (Too Bad)/Lick And A Promise/Big Ten Inch Record/Dream On [*]/Lord Of The Thighs [*]
Side 2: Last Child/Walk This Way/Same Old Song And Dance/Train Kept A Rollin'/Get The Lead Out/Batman Theme/Toys In The Attic
Recorded: Budokan, Tokyo, February 9, 1977, except [*] January 31, 1977.
Cover: Red deluxe.
Quality: Very good mono.
Comments: Japanese origin.

AEROSMITH LIVE (Cassette) 1977
Side 1: Mama Kin/SOS (Too Bad)/Big Ten Inch Record/Lord Of The Thighs/Lick And A Promise/Dream On/Walkin' The Dog
Side 2: Sweet Emotion/Walk This Way/Draw The Line/Same Old Song And Dance/Train Kept A Rollin'/Toys In The Attic
Recorded: Reading Festival, England, August 1977.

Quality: Very good.
Comments: Only known bootleg from Aerosmith's two European tours in the seventies; includes preview version of 'Draw The Line'.

THE HARD WAY (Ruthless Rhymes) 1977
Side 1: Back In The Saddle/Big Ten Inch Record/I Wanna Know Why/Get It Up/Walk This Way/Sweet Emotion
Side 2: Dream On/Walkin' The Dog/Draw The Line/Same Old Song And Dance/Train Kept A Rollin'
Recorded: Las Vegas, Nevada, November 25, 1977.
Cover: Pale blue live pic of Tyler.
Quality: Very good stereo.
Comments: One of the most common Aerosmith bootlegs.

GET YOUR LEAD OUT MAMA! (Unknown) 1978
Side 1: Rats In The Cellar/I Wanna Know Why/Big Ten Inch Record/Walk This Way/Sight For Sore Eyes/Seasons Of Wither/Sweet Emotion
Side 2: Lord Of The Thighs/Dream On/Chip Away The Stone/Get The Lead Out/Get It Up/Draw The Line/Same Old Song And Dance/Toys In The Attic/Milk Cow Blues/Train Kept A Rollin'
Recorded: Columbus, Ohio, 1978.
Cover: Deluxe purple with live shot of Tyler against white background; duplicated band logo on right.
Quality: Excellent mono.
Comments: One of the author's favourites!

LIVE IN NEW YORK (KHS 2598) 1978
Side 1: School Boy/Somebody/Dream On/Need Love/Walk This Way
Side 2: Train Kept A Rollin'/Toys In The Attic/Train Kept A Rollin' (reprise)
Recorded: New York, 1978.
Cover: Pink, deluxe.
Quality: Fair mono.
Comments: 'School Boy' is actually 'SOS (Too Bad)', and 'Need Love' is also incorrectly identified.

PURE GOLD .999 (P&E Records 001) 1979
Side 1: Bolivian Ragamuffin/Bitches Brew (instrumental)/Bolivian Ragamuffin/Hey You

Side 2: The Jig Is Up/Jailbait/Lightning Strikes/Joanie's Butterfly (instrumental)/Cry Me A River
Recorded: Criteria Studios, Miami, Florida, 1979.
Cover: Deluxe black and gold, with band logo.
Quality: Excellent stereo.
Comments: Out-takes from the recording of 'Rock In A Hard Place', with Tyler ad-libbing vocals on some tracks. Of European origin, the first 50 pressings were on coloured vinyl and came with a booklet.

AEROSMITH LIVE (Cassette) 1983
Side 1: Back In The Saddle/Big Ten Inch Record/Mama Kin/Three Mile Smile/Reefer Head Woman/Lord Of The Thighs/No More No More/Lick And A Promise/Sick As A Dog
Side 2: Sweet Emotion/Dream On/Same Old Song And Dance/Walk This Way/Milk Cow Blues/Toys In The Attic/Train Kept A Rollin'
Recorded: Cal Expo Amphitheatre, Sacramento, California, August 2, 1983.
Quality: Excellent.
Comments: Only known live bootleg of Crespo/Dufay line-up.

STONE COLD (Pharting Pharaoh Records 13157) 1986
Side 1: Back In The Saddle/Rats In The Cellar/Big Ten Inch Record/My Fist Your Face/Last Child
Side 2: Three Mile Smile/Red House/Lord Of The Thighs/Mama Kin/Sweet Emotion
Side 3: Guitar Improvisation/Walk This Way/Let The Music Do The Talking/Drum Solo/Toys In The Attic
Side 4: Honky Tonk Woman/Dream On/Your Lover Needs Lovin'/Stone Cold Blues/Train Kept A Rollin'
Recorded: San Francisco, January 24, 1986.
Cover: Deluxe colour with deluxe label.
Quality: Good-to-very-good stereo.
Comments: Includes rare version of The Stones' 'Honky Tonk Woman'.

AEROSMITH LIVE (Cassette) 1986
Side 1: Back In The Saddle/Same Old Song And Dance/Bone To Bone/Big Ten Inch Record/My Fist Your Face/Last Child/Shame On You/Mother Popcorn/No Surprise/She's On Fire
Side 2: Walkin' The Dog/The Hop/Red House/Lightning Strikes/Sheila/Walk This Way/Let The Music Do The Talking
Recorded: Philadelphia, August 3, 1986.
Quality: Very good.
Comments: From the 'Done With Mirrors' tour.

AERODYNAMICS (A–71116/621) 1986/87
Side 1: Bone To Bone/Dude (Looks Like A Lady)/Big Ten Inch Record/Walk This Way
Side 2: Joe Perry Solo/Draw The Line/Rag Doll/Dream On/Sweet Emotion
Side 3: Same Old Song And Dance/Back In The Saddle/My Fist Your Face/Last Child/No Surprise/She's On Fire
Side 4: The Hop/Red House/Let The Music Do The Talking/Toys In The Attic/Train Kept A Rollin'
Recorded: Sides 1 and 2 at the Civic Centre, Hampton, Vancouver, November 16, 1987; sides 3 and 4 at the Orange Pavilion, San Bernadino, California, February 1, 1986.
Cover: Deluxe brown and white.
Quality: Sides 1 and 2 excellent stereo; sides 3 and 4 excellent mono.
Comments: Japanese origin, 300 pressed.

WHEN THE LIGHTNING STRIKES (Pharting Pharaoh Records 13166) 1988
Side 1: Toys In The Attic/Same Old Song And Dance/Come Back/Dude (Looks Like A Lady)/Big Ten Inch Record
Side 2: When The Lightning Strikes/Rag Doll/Hangman Jury/Permanent Vacation/Angel
Side 3: Back In The Saddle/Brad Solo-man/Last Child/Joe Fucking Perry Solo/Draw The Line/Dream On
Side 4: Train Kept A Rollin'/Sweet Emotion/Joe And Brad The Blues Brothers/I'm Down/Walk This Way
Recorded: Long Beach Arena, Los Angeles, February 6, 1988.
Cover: Deluxe cover and label with 'Permanent Vacation' graphics surrounding pic of lace-clad model with sparkler fireworks attached to small dumb-bell weights.
Quality: Very good/excellent stereo.
Comments: 'Come Back' is actually 'Bone To Bone (Coney Island White Fish Boy)'; also includes snippets of 'One Way Street' and 'Darkness'.

PUSSY 'N' BOOZE (This West Production Company) 1988
Mama Kin
Recorded: Pacific Amphitheatre, September 15, 1988.
Cover: Pink pic sleeve.
Quality: Very good.
Comments: One track from a Guns n' Roses bootleg, a jam between the two bands during the Aerosmith/Guns n' Roses US tour.